PAPER FOLDING FOR BEGINNERS

(formerly titled: Fun with Paper Folding)

by

WILLIAM D. MURRAY

and

FRANCIS J. RIGNEY

Dover Publications, Inc.
New York   York

Foreword

FOR many years I have entertained people, young and old, with paper. Once it was a group of soldiers and nurses crossing the Adriatic, among them some Greeks on the way to represent their country at Versailles, one of whom suggested an improvement in the bird I had been making. Another time it was in a box car in which I was riding from Changsha to Hankow, China, crowded with desolate, ragged soldiers. Again it was in the great marble stadium at Athens with a group of Greek Boy Scouts. In every case and among all these different kinds of people, interest was aroused, and pleasant hours passed.

Generally, however, my opportunities have come when I have been able to meet a group of children, as at Silver Bay. Sometimes it has been one or two children on a train. But always it has allayed restlessness, and helped through the day.

While some of the objects may seem difficult a little practice has been found the only thing needed. A great many children have learned to make most of the objects described in the book. One little girl who learned to make and tell the paper folding story, gave it as one of the numbers at the Christmas entertainment, in her Sunday-school in Shanghai.

From time to time I have heard from readers who have amplified the designs or who suggest others not now found in our book. I should be very glad to have sent to me in care of the publishers any suggestions from those who are using the book, which may be incorporated in new editions, with the personal acknowledgment of the author.

The book is intended for children, of course, but parents and friends of children will soon discover that ability to make these simple objects will afford entertainment to young and old and will be very helpful on many different occasions.

New York City

W. D. M.

This Dover edition, first published in 1960, is a revised version of the work originally published by Fleming H. Revell Company in 1928 under the title *Fun with Paper Folding*.

Standard Book Number: 486-20713-7
Library of Congress Catalog Card Number: 61-1450

Manufactured in the United States of America
Dover Publications, Inc., 180 Varick Street, New York 10014

Contents

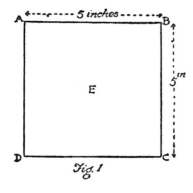

Fig. 1

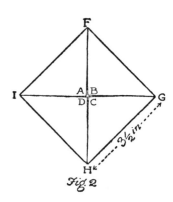

Fig. 2

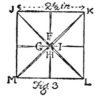

Fig. 3

Fig. 3a

Fig. 4

Fig. 4a

Paper Folding

There are two ways of starting to fold paper, depending upon what is to be made.

THE FIRST METHOD

The paper may be of any size but must be perfectly square. It should be paper that will not tear easily, bond paper for instance. In all our descriptions here we will use a five-inch square, as it is a convenient size.

First let us fold the paper in order to get the creases necessary in making the various toys or objects. With the five-inch square of paper flat on the table fold the corners A. B. C. and D. (Fig. 1) to E. the centre, being careful to have each point fall on the exact centre. (Success depends very largely upon the care with which the folds are made.) This centre can be determined by folding B. over on D., opening out and folding C. over on A. The fold from A. to C. will cross the fold from B. to D. exactly at the centre E.

When the corners A. B. C. D. have been folded into the centre (Fig. 2) turn the paper over so that the folded corners are on the underside next the table. Now fold the new points F. G. H. I. upward and in to the centre X. (Fig. 3), which is on the reverse side from centre E. Turn over Fig. 3, still folded, so that the centre E. (covered by A. B. C. D.), is again uppermost (Fig. 3a). Fold the new corners, J. K. L. M. into the centre. The new square is Fig. 4. The reverse side is Fig. 4a. The square will now be one and three-quarters of an inch in size. The paper is now so creased that many toys or objects can be made with it. There follow descriptions of some of these.

THE SALT CELLAR

This is the simplest object to make. Sometimes it is called the pig's foot. This is simply the folds in the first and second steps (Fig. 3a). Squeeze the paper down along the lines from the corners J. K. L. M. (Fig. 5) to the centre E. so that E. will point at the top and the corners J. K. L. M. will come together at the bottom (Fig. 6). Looking down upon the folded paper it will appear shaped like the letter X.

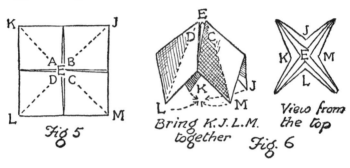

Fig 5

Bring K. J. L. M. together

View from the top *Fig. 6*

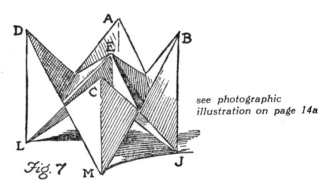

Fig. 7

see photographic illustration on page 14a

The four flaps A. B. C. D. meeting at E. can now be opened out (Fig. 7), and if desired folded all the way down, or in, on points J. K. L. M. This is the salt cellar. Turn it upside down and it is a pig's foot, or, as some prefer to call it, a nose pincher.

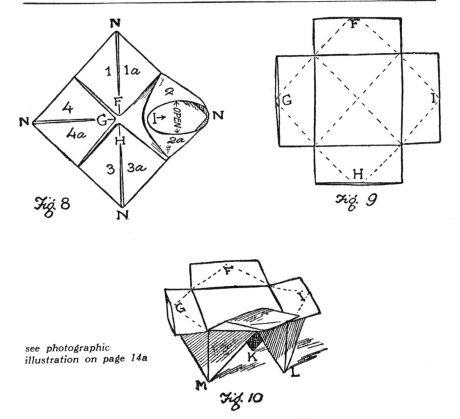

Fig. 8

Fig. 9

see photographic
illustration on page 14a

Fig. 10

THE CAKE BASKET

To make the cake basket take the paper when folded as in
Fig. 8 (enlarged drawing of 4a) and one by one open out the
little squares 1, 2, 3, and 4 causing 1 and 1a to part—sketch
shows 2 and 2a partly opened out. When the four squares are
opened the points F. G. H. and I. will each rest on the corners
N. N. N. N. The folded paper will now look like Fig. 9. Underneath will be found the four feet on which the cake basket stands
(Points J. K. L. M.). Bend these points out so that the basket
will stand up (Fig. 10).

THE SHIRT WAIST

Take the cake basket, fold the legs J. K. L. M. together underneath (Fig. 10) and open out the two opposite folds G. and I. (Fig. 11 shows I. opened out). Fold back and bend down the points G. and I. as shown in Fig. 12. These points make the sleeves, while F. makes the collar and H. the waist band.

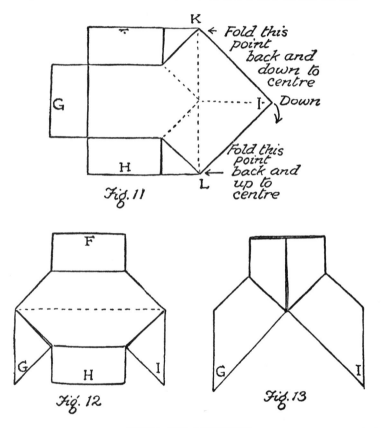

Fig. 11 *Fig. 12* *Fig. 13*

THE TROUSERS

Fold H. over on F. along the dotted line shown in Fig. 12 letting I. and G. form the legs and H. the waist (Fig. 13).

12

THE MOTOR-BOAT

Take the trousers (Fig. 13) and turn the corners G. and I. inside out and up. There will be two funnels one beside the other (H. and F. of Fig. 14). G. is the bow and I. the stern. G. and I. can be easily spread and pulled out until the boat is shown as in Fig. 15.

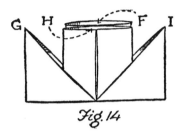

Fig. 14

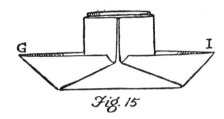

Fig. 15

THE TABLE

Fold the paper three times to get the creases, as described in first paragraph (Figs. 2, 3, and 4), fold it with the first fold only (Fig. 2). Because of the creases made by the other folds the paper will look as in Fig. 16. Squeeze M. and L. together to meet in the centre and so that the point H. sticks up. In the same way bring points J. and K. to the centre. This will form Fig. 17. Turn over and the table is made, F. G. H. and I. forming the legs.

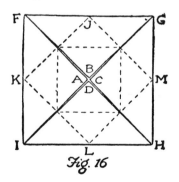

Fig. 16

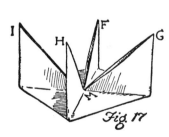

Fig. 17

THE WINDMILL

By bending over the legs of the table and pressing them down flat you make the windmill (Fig. 18).

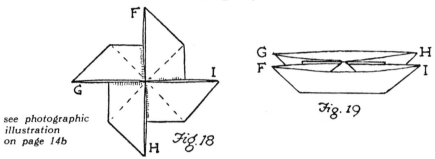

see photographic illustration on page 14b

Fig. 18

Fig. 19

THE DOUBLE ROWBOAT

With the paper folded as a table, instead of folding across diagonally, fold across the top of the table so as to bring two opposite sides of the square together. Then push what were the legs of the table, two by two, so that they form bows and sterns as in Fig. 19.

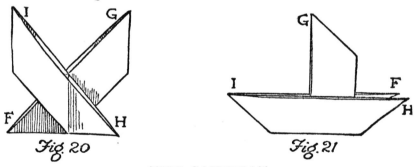

Fig. 20

Fig. 21

THE SAILBOAT

Turn the table (Fig. 17) upside down, take hold of two opposite feet say H. and F., bend them back and down. This folds the top diagonally so that the paper comes out like Fig. 20 with the former table legs sticking out at F. and H. and at I. and G. Turn the point F. back against H. and you get the sailboat Fig. 21).

14

Plate I The Salt Cellar (see page 10) and The Cake Basket (see page 11).

Plate II The Windmill (see page 14), The Rooster (see page 15), and The Work Table (see page 18).

THE ROOSTER

Take the sailboat (Fig. 21). Turn the bow of the boat I. inside out and down (Fig. 22). Turn the paper until it rests on the two legs F. and H. and on the tail G. Put in a dot for an eye (Fig. 23).

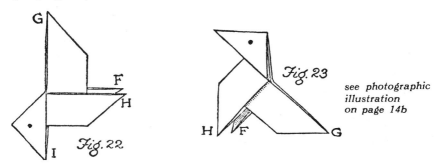

Fig. 22 *Fig. 23*

see photographic illustration on page 14b

THE POCKET BOOK

Proceed from the double boat (Fig. 19). Inside F. I. will be found a flap F. A. I. (Fig. 24). Pull this flap out and fold points F. A. and I. so that each rests on K. You will then have Fig. 25 showing points H. and G. of second boat at the back. Similarly fold G. and H. and point of flap C. each down on point A. at the back of the paper. You will then have two envelope-like squares back to back (Fig. 26). Fold each square through centre along the dotted line so that the top edge in each case rests on the bottom edge. This makes the pocketbook (Fig. 27).

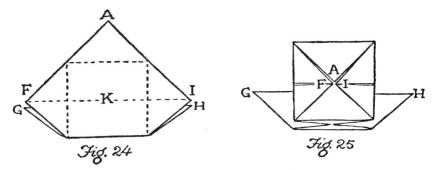

Fig. 24 *Fig. 25*

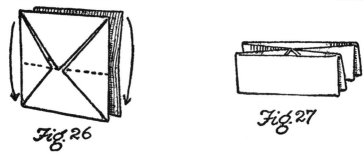

THE CAP

Continuing from the pocketbook pull gently on the two outer flaps and the paper will open out and will be like a square box open on the top. Turn it upside down to make the cap and extend one of the flaps to make the cap's peak (Fig. 28). Turn the other flap inward.

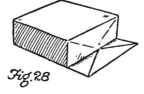

THE CHINESE JUNK

Make a square box, as described in making the cap (Fig. 28). Looking down on the open side it will appear as in Fig. 29. Fold the side marked L. along the dotted line squeezing inward in the direction of the arrow. Do likewise with the side marked J. The paper will then be as in Fig. 30. Then fold the two flap sides back until the top edges of the squeezed sides J. and L. form straight lines and the under edges of the same sides fold as shown in Fig. 31. The top of the folded paper will now look like a picture frame (Fig. 32). Fold back the paper in half until the edges J. and L. meet. The under side will now look like Fig. 33 and the side view like Fig. 34. Hold firmly at point B. (Fig. 34) and gently pull out the corners X. X., one at a time taking care not to tear the paper. The points will come up level with the edge J. and you will have the Chinese Junk (Fig. 35). The diamond shapes at each end are flaps which may be pulled up to form awnings, underneath which will be found the end seats (Fig. 36).

16

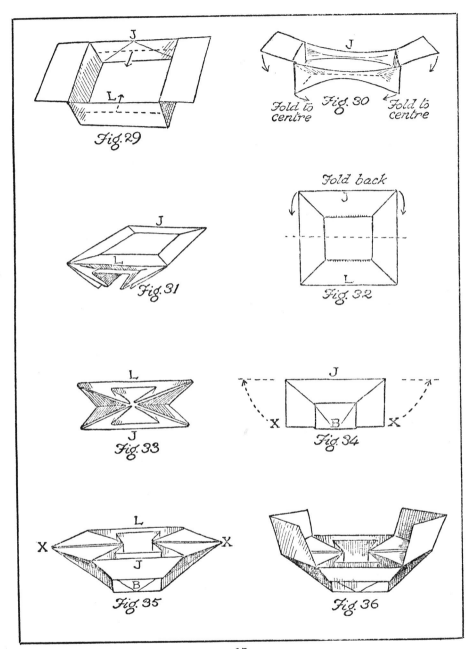

J

I

L↑

Fig. 29

J

Fold to centre   Fig. 30   Fold to centre

Fold back

J

L

Fig. 32

J

L

Fig. 31

L

J

Fig. 33

J

X   B   X

Fig. 34

L

X   J   X

B

Fig. 35

Fig. 36

17

THE WORK TABLE

Start with Fig. 37 (Fig. 2 in creasing). Fold backward along dotted line L. J. with open side out until point F. is on G. and I. is on H. as in Fig. 38. Fold point J. over on M. and fold point L. in a similar manner but backwards on point K. on the reverse side. You will now have Fig. 39. Open from H. to G. in the centre and push the two points together to form Fig. 40. Open from F. to B. and push point F. up to B. You then get Fig. 41. Fold back along dotted line so that the edge F. coincides with the line J. K. making the triangles X. X. and you get Fig. 42. Fold in similar manner on the other side of the paper. Fold along the dotted line B. F. so that the two triangles X. and X. come together. Do the same on both sides and form Fig. 43. Fold the points A. and D. back on the dotted lines and so with the points B. and C. on the other side so that you will have four points

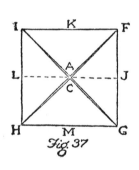

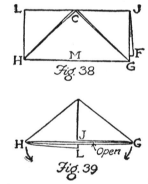

around the central point E. (Fig. 44). Fold along the dotted lines extending from A. and D. so that the sides K. and L. will both coincide with the line from E. to I. Repeat on the other side. You will then have Fig. 45. Fold along dotted line so that point I. fits in exactly between points K. and L. Repeat on the other side and you will have Fig. 46. Fold along X. X. so that point X¹. X¹. will fall on points X². X². Repeat on the other side and the paper will be as in Fig. 47. Turn upside down and push open in the centre the point E. into the centre. You will then have your work table, with leaves on each side (Fig. 48).

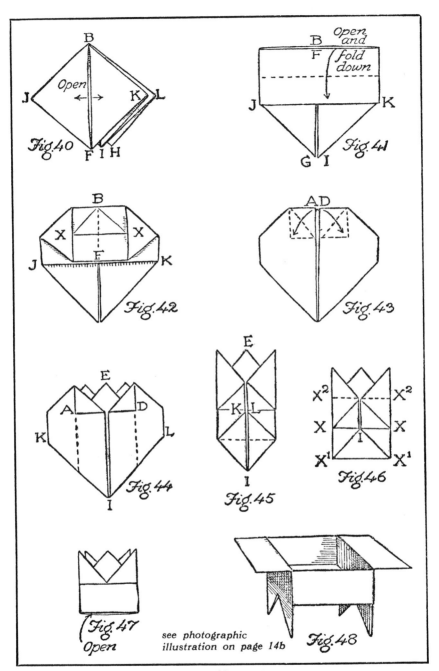

Fig.40 — Open

Fig.41 — Open and fold down

Fig.42

Fig.43

Fig.44

Fig.45

Fig.46

Fig.47 — Open

see photographic
illustration on page 14b

Fig.48

THE BATTLESHIP

Start with Fig. 49 (this is Fig. 3a of the folding for creases). With the paper thus fold M. up to K. Pull B. and D. out so that they stand up as shown in Fig. 50. Now open the line from H. G. to M. Bending M. down so that it will rest on H. G. The triangle of which M. was the top point will now open out into an oblong (Fig. 51). Tuck the two lower corners of this X. X. in behind the triangles G. B. J. and H. L. D. You will then have Fig. 52, the dotted line showing where X. X. had been tucked behind. Repeat on the reverse side bringing down point K. and opening it out as with point M.

Now comes the difficulty. The points B. and D. must be pulled down and turned out. Fig. 53 shows point B. partly turned over. Be careful not to tear the paper. Keep at it until practice and patience make perfect. When both ends have been turned out and down the paper will look like Fig. 54. Inside of the oblong in the centre will be found two flaps which you pull out and push back into the openings which they were covering. There will then be three openings or pockets, one each side of the central opening. Cut a piece of paper an inch and a half square, fold it and insert one side in each of the side pockets of the oblong (Fig. 55). Before inserting this piece of new paper

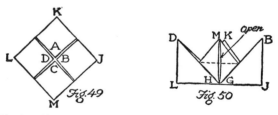

make two little slits along the line of the fold, a little way apart from each other. Roll two little pieces of paper, about one inch by half an inch, flatting one end of each roll and insert the flat ends in the slits for funnels. Make slits on each side of the bow and stern (B. and D.) as indicated, and insert two rolls (like the funnels, but not quite so large), at each end, for the guns. The completed battleship is Fig. 56.

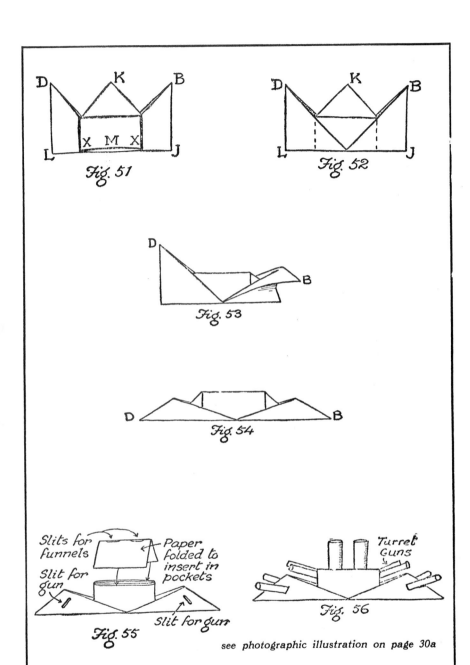

Fig. 51

Fig. 52

Fig. 53

Fig. 54

Slits for funnels
Paper folded to insert in pockets
Slit for gun
Slit for gun

Fig. 55

Turret Guns

Fig. 56

see photographic illustration on page 30a

THE DOG

Fig. 57. Make three small shirtwaists (See Fig. 12). A small dog looks better than a large one. Turn one shirtwaist A. over and arrange the three as shown. Insert B. in A. and C. in B. Turn 1, 2, 3 and 4 down and perpendicular to B. and C. and they will form the legs of the dog. 5 and 6 turned up will be his ears and A. is the head and B. and C. form the body. Put two dots on A. to make his eyes. X. is his nose and Y. his stubby tail.

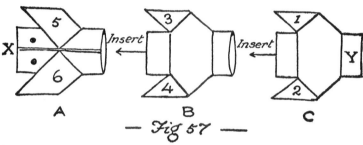

see photographic illustration on page 30a

THE HOUSE

Fold the paper as shown at the beginning of the book all the way from Fig. 1 to 4a. The paper will then when opened out flat be creased as in Fig. 58. With a scissors cut along the heavy lines removing the little triangles marked 'X' and cut into each Y. as shown in Fig. 59. Cut slits at the bases of the two triangles A. and B. Cut two little squares or windows on the lines Y. M. and a door in the triangle K. as indicated. Bend up each of the little squares F. G. H. and I. The central square Y. Y. Y. Y. with E. in the middle is the floor of the house and the oblongs J. K. L. and M. bent on the lines Y. Y. perpendicular to the bottom, are the sides. Fig. 60 shows the paper partly folded. Insert the flaps C. and D. through the opposite slits A. and B. and you will have the house (Fig. 61).

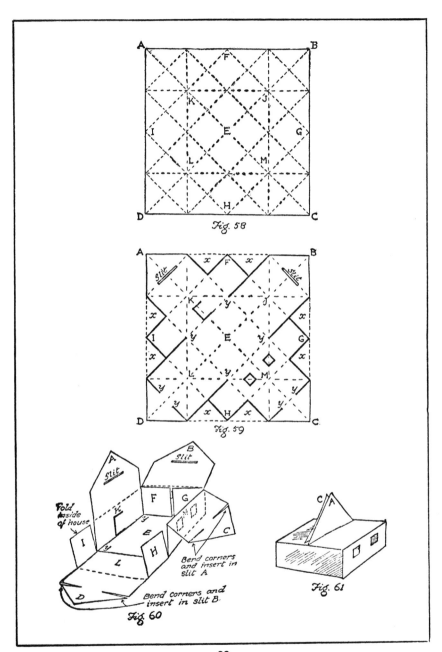

Fig. 58

Fig. 59

Fold inside of house

Bend corners and insert in slit A

Bend corners and insert in slit B.

Fig. 60

Fig. 61

23

II

Diagonal Folding

THE SECOND METHOD

The second way to fold the paper for creasing purposes is to take the square, fold it diagonally on one side, from A. to B., and from C. to D. The folds will cross on the centre E. (Fig. 62). Open the paper out, turn it over, and on the opposite side fold the edge B. C. over on A. D., and opening it out, again fold B. D. over on C. A. You then have the paper with diagonal creases on one side and with rectangular creases on the other (Fig. 63). With the creases from F. to H. and from I. to G. folding downwards, and the diagonal creases pushing up from the back, this side of the paper looks like a four-pointed star. Make the creases hard. When turned over the centre point will be highest and the paper assumes a more or less spear point shape.

THE BALL

Start as described above. With Fig. 63 side upwards bring the points I. and G. together so that you have two triangles J. B. D. and J. C. A. one behind the other, as in Fig. 64. Fold points B. and D. up to J. on the dotted lines H. L. and H. K. (Fig. 65). Repeat on the other side with points C. and A. You will now have Fig. 66. Fold points L. and K. along the dotted lines so that the two points meet on the line J. H. (Fig. 67). Repeat on the other side with points M. and N. Now fold down point D. and tuck it in as far as it will go into the opening of the little triangle K. Fold point B. in a similar manner into triangle L. Repeat on the other side (Fig. 68). It will be found that there is a small opening at the bottom H. Open out the paper so that as you look down on it, it looks like an X., cover the hole at H. with the mouth and blow gently. This will inflate the ball (Fig. 69).

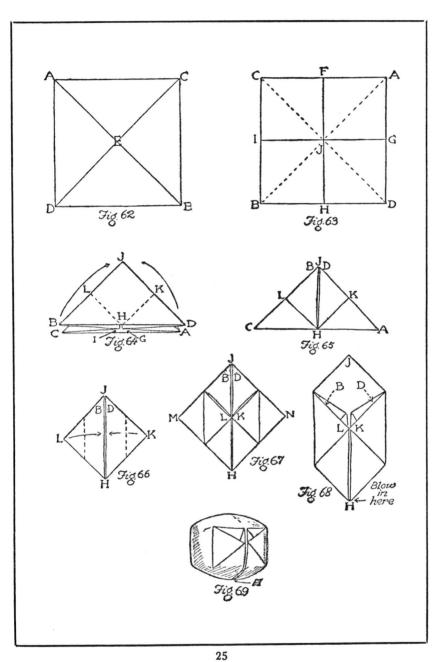

Fig. 62

Fig. 63

Fig. 64

Fig. 65

Fig. 66

Fig. 67

Fig. 68

Blow
in
here

Fig. 69

THE SUGAR BOWL

Proceed as far as Fig. 67 in the ball. There will be found four triangles, two on one side (L. and K.), and two on the other side (M. and N.). Treat each one alike. Turn back K. to its position where it was before, making the small triangle (Fig. 70). Then unfold point D. along the line H. K. and make the triangle J. H. D. (Fig. 71). Now fold point D. over the dotted line X. X., so that K. will come to point L. (Fig. 72). Push up the lower point X. so that the paper will fold along the dotted line and so that D. will turn over and point X. fall on the line H. J., making a small triangle (Fig. 73).

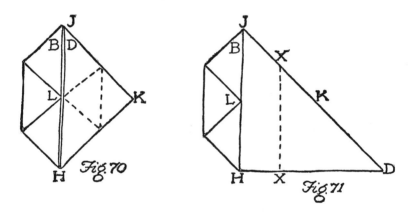

Fold D. back over triangle X. (Fig. 74). When point B. and points A. and C. at the back of the paper have all been treated in the same way, two of the points will form a handle on one side and two a handle on the other side (Fig. 75). There will be a small opening at H. as in the ball. Hold by the handles and inflate (Fig. 76). This is Fig. 75 inflated and turned upside down.

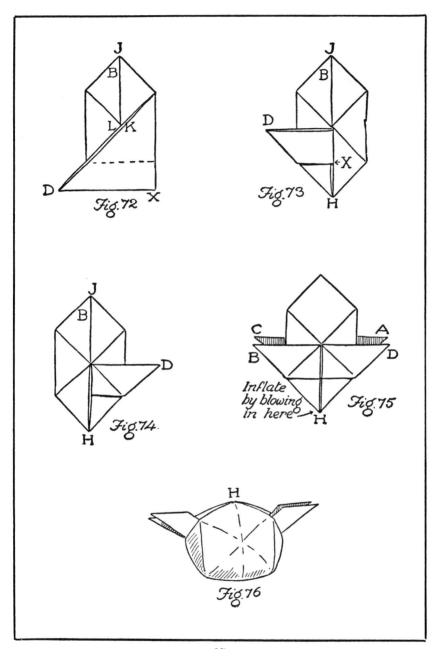

Fig. 72

Fig. 73

Fig. 74.

Inflate
by blowing
in here→

Fig. 75

Fig. 76

THE BIRD

With E side of the paper turned up as in Fig. 62, fold the paper so that the lines A. E., B. E., C. E. and D. E. come together, the points A. B. C. and D. all meeting at the bottom. It will then be somewhat like a closed umbrella. Then flatten the paper with two folds on each side (Fig. 77). Fold the edge G. A. along the dotted line until the point G. rests on the line A. E. Fold F. A. on the dotted line until point F. meets point G. Repeat with points H. and I. on the other side and you will have Fig. 78. Then open out points F. and G. and push point A. up so that the paper will fold up and back on the line F. G. Fig. 79 shows paper opened and point A. on its way up. This will bring the points F. G. together again on a line A. B. and you will have Fig. 80. This latter folding may take a little practice to perfect. Repeat on the other side, bringing point B. up to A. Now fold points A. and B. down again on opposite sides so that they rest on points C. and D. (Fig. 81). Turn the paper on its side and it will look as in Fig. 82, with fold E. D. running down the middle. Now comes the difficult part. Again practice and patience. Holding the paper firmly on both sides at spot marked Y., pull out the point D. and pinch the two upper edges X. X. together (Fig. 83). There will be a small V-shaped crease just above each point X. Bend X. X. in direction of arrow back into space under E. so that point D. will stick up as in Fig. 84. Do the same with point C. on the other side and you will have Fig. 85. Fold point A. up on the dotted line. Do the same with point B. on the other side. A. and B. are the tip ends of the bird's wings (Fig. 86). Bend point D. down, as shown, to make the bird's head. Put a dot on each side for the eyes. C. is the tail. Hold at X. and roll the wings, as if making a cornucopia, with the small end away from the head (Fig. 87). This roll is just to get a bend in the wings and it will curve the wing tips forward toward the head. Stretch the bird's head out to a flying position. With thumb hold firmly at X. Gently pull the bird's tail. This will cause the wings to flap (Fig. 88).

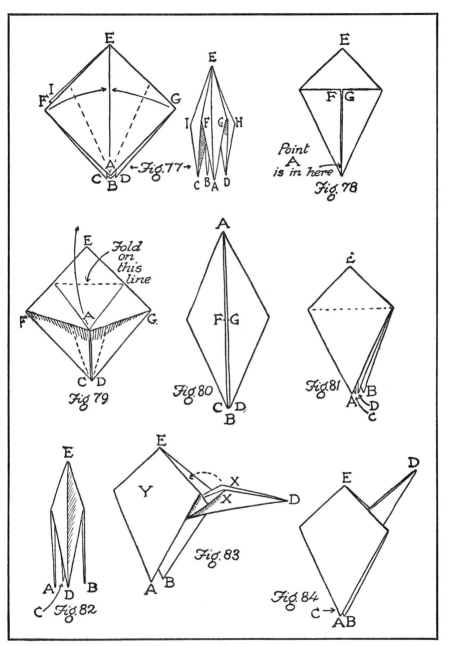

E

F I   G

A

C B D   ←*Fig.77*→

E

I F G H

C B A D

E

F G

Point
A
is in here

Fig. 78

E   *Fold*
on
this
line

F   A   G

C D

Fig 79

A

F G

C D
B

Fig 80

E

B
A D
C

Fig 81

E

A D B
C

Fig 82

E

Y   X
X   D

A B

Fig. 83

D

E

C → A B

Fig. 84

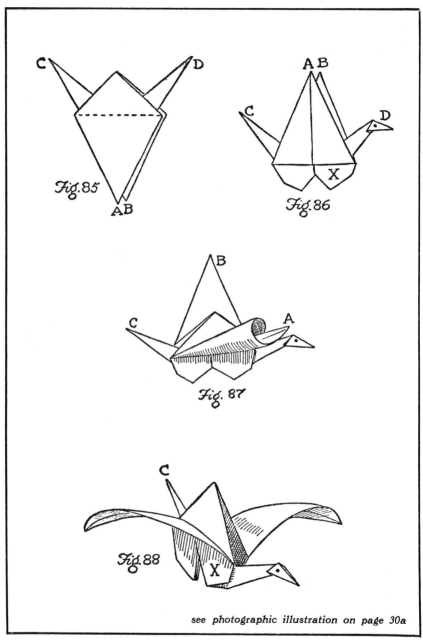

Fig.85

Fig.86

Fig. 87

Fig.88

see photographic illustration on page 30a

30

Plate III The Battleship (see page 20), The Dog (see page 22), and The Bird (see page 28).

Plate IV The Frog (see page 31), The Pagoda (see page 34), and The Boat (see page 41).

THE FROG

Begin with the paper folded having E. again as uppermost point as in making the bird. There will be four projecting points, F. G. H. and I. (Fig. 89). Open out and flatten down each of these points on the centre line, as in Fig. 90. When all four points have been flattened down you will have Fig. 91. Fold the line K. C. over so that it will coincide with F. C., and treat L. A. the same way, so that it coincides with F. A. (Fig. 92). You will then have two new points M. and N. Partly open out points K. and L. Push point F. up causing the paper to fold back on the line M. N. Points K. and L. will come together and you will then have Fig. 93. There will be three

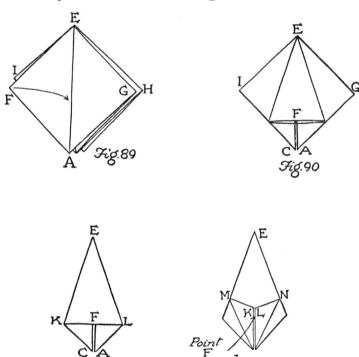

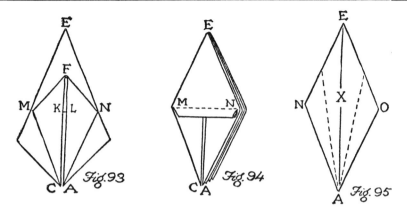

other sides to treat in this way, points G. H. and I. going up as did point F. Select any one of the four folded up points, say point F., and roll it down hard (Fig. 94). This strengthens the frog's back. There will then be four edges on each side at E. N. and at E. M. Fig. 94 shows the E. N. side. Now open out the first space immediately behind point N. The paper will now look like Fig. 95. Fold points N. and O. along the dotted line, so that they meet on the centre line at point X. This will require careful folding as the space begins to narrow. You now get Fig. 96. Do the same on the E. M. side. There will be two others looking like Fig. 95. Fold them inward as were the corners in Fig. 96 and they will appear as in Fig. 97. Now turn the paper around until you come to the side which shows where it was rolled down between points M. and N. in Fig. 94. It will be as in Fig. 98, and there will be four separate points at the bottom, two on top and two underneath. The four points sticking down are the frog's legs, and the part marked X. is the frog's back. Fold the upper two at an acute angle and then fold each twice again as shown in Fig. 99. Fold the two lower legs at right angles to the body (Fig. 100), and repeat extra folds as in the first case. Cover the four legs and part of the body with the mouth and inflate through the opening at the lower end.

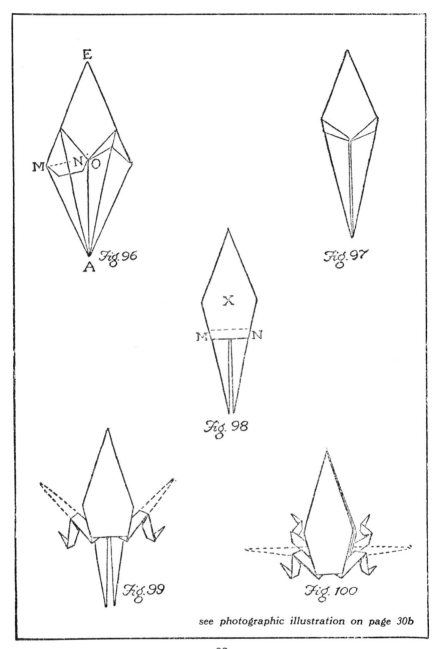

Fig. 96

Fig. 97

Fig. 98

Fig. 99

Fig. 100

see photographic illustration on page 30b

THE PAGODA

Take five or six squares of paper of various sizes, e.g., five inches, four and a half inches, four inches, three and a half inches, and three inches. Begin with the five inch square, and fold as in Fig. 101. (This is Fig. 64 in the making of the ball.) Fold point D. up on J. along the line H. K. Fold B. in like manner. Do the same with points C. and A. at the back. Fig. 102 shows the manner of folding. There will then be four triangles like D. K. H. and B. L. H. two on each side. Open triangle D. K. H. so that D. comes to H. Fig. 103 shows point D. coming down. This folding forms a square D. M. K. N. (Fig. 104). Do the same with the other three triangles. Turn the paper so that it folds on the dotted line J. H. bringing the sides K. N. and L. P. together. Repeat with two squares on the other side. You will then have Fig. 105. Fold the side L. P. along dotted line X. X. so that L. P. falls along the line J. I. Do the same with the other three sides corresponding to L. P. You will then have Fig. 106. Now fold X. and X. on each other. Repeat on the other side and form Fig. 107. The two oblongs Y. and Y. thus formed will be found to open on their inner edges along the centre line J. H. Push the point H. at the bottom upward until the oblongs Y. and Y. open out on each side, and the point H. folds back on the centre of the paper as in Fig. 108. Do the same on the other side. Fold Y. over on Y. along the centre dotted line and you will have Fig. 109. Repeat on the other side. Turn back each of the four corners along the dotted diagonal lines of the squares so the bottom outside corners X^1. and X^2. fold up to X. (Fig. 110). Now spread out the four corners so that they point North, South, East and West. This forms the base of the pagoda. Treat each square of paper in the same way and stand them one on top of the other. They will fit together. As many pieces can be made as may be desired. The whole will form the pagoda (Fig. 111).

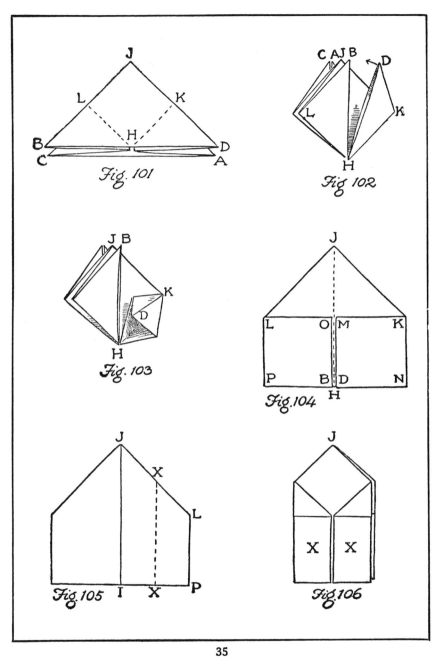

Fig. 101

Fig. 102

Fig. 103

Fig. 104

Fig. 105

Fig. 106

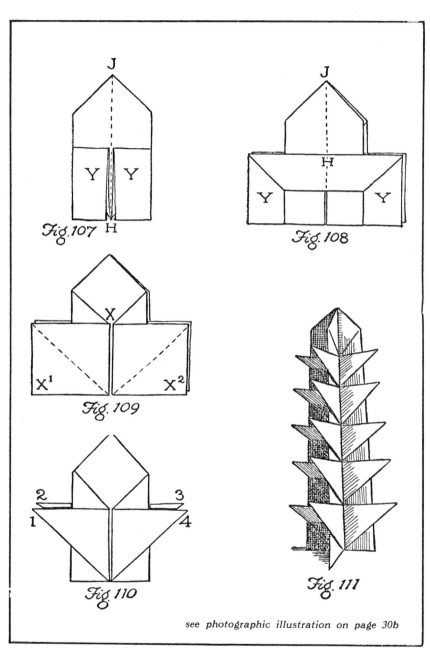

Fig. 107

Fig. 108

Fig. 109

Fig. 110

Fig. 111

see *photographic illustration on page 30b*

THE AIRPLANE

Take two pieces of paper, one a square five inches by five inches, and the other a strip about ten inches long by two inches wide. Fold the square as for the pagoda (Fig. 101), that is, where the points B. and D. fold up to and meet on J., leaving the points A. and C. untouched. Now fold on the dotted lines (Fig. 112) points X. and X., so that they meet on the centre line J. H. This is done so as to get a crease on the dotted line. You now have Fig. 113. Open out and then fold in a similar

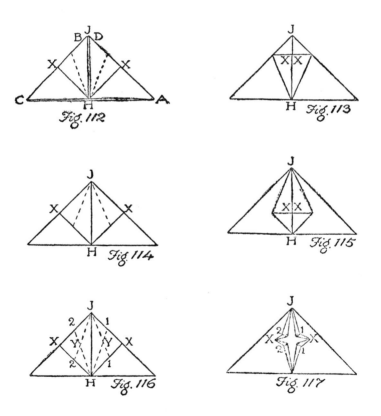

Fig. 112

Fig. 113

Fig. 114

Fig. 115

Fig. 116

Fig. 117

manner, but in the other direction on the diamond **X. J. X. H.**, that is along the dotted line (Fig. 114). When you do this the points **X. X.** will again meet on the centre line, but this time down in the direction of **H.** (Fig. 115). Open out once more and you will have four creased lines (Fig. 116). Where the lines cross in each case at **Y.**, pinch the paper 1 to 1 and 2 to 2, so that you will get a crease running out from **Y.** to **X.** This will cause the paper to fold as shown in Fig. 117, the points **X.** and **X.** sticking up. Bring the pinched points **X.** and **X.** together and fold them back in the direction of **J.** (Fig. 118).

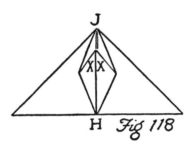

Now take the long strip of paper and fold it along the centre lengthways, this makes a crease which stiffens the paper. Open this fold out and turn in two corners on one end to meet on crease as shown in Fig. 119. Now insert this pointed slip under **H.** in Fig. 118 and push all the way up to **J.** (Fig. 120). Having done this bend back point **J.** along the dotted line **Y. Y.**, so that **J.** goes underneath and points **X.** and **X.** are out in front. Now fold up, at right angles to the strip, a small piece of the tail, about a quarter of an inch, and cut this in the centre as shown in Fig. 121. You now have the airplane . Hold at **J.** underneath and throw smoothly. The plane will glide and will turn either side depending upon the arrangement of the two little folds at the cut end, one fold sticking up and one remaining flat. Crease the wings up slightly.

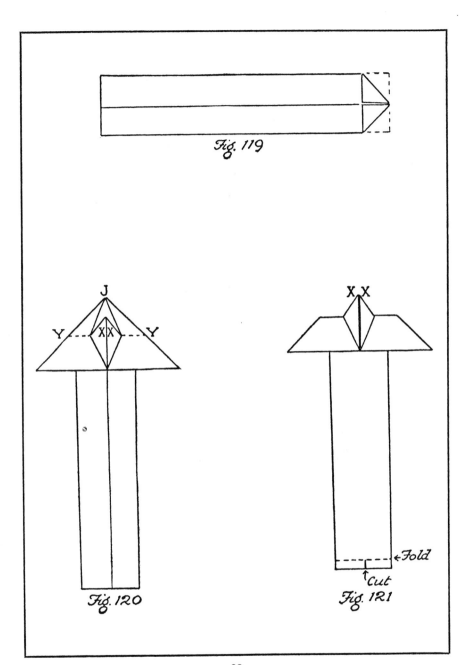

Fig. 119

Fig. 120

Fig. 121

←Fold

↑Cut

III

Miscellaneous Folding

The following objects do not come under either of the previous methods of creasing and folding and are of a miscellaneous character.

THE DRINKING CUP

Take a square of paper and fold on one diagonal (Fig. 122). The distance from A. to G. is about two-fifths of the base line A. B. of the triangle A. B. C. Fold point A. over on F. along dotted line E. G. Fold B. over on E. You will then have Fig. 123. The line B. F. will be parallel to G. H. Now fold point C.—there will be two points at the top, fold only the front one—down into the front pocket of triangle B. F. H. Squeeze the sides B. G. and F. H. and the cup will open out. This cup may be used for drinking.

Make large enough and turn in the point which was behind C. and you will have a paper hat. Dent the hat in the top. The bottom of the cup then becomes the top of the hat.

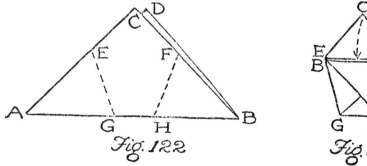

Fig. 122

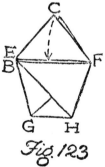

Fig. 123

THE BOAT

Take a piece of paper A. B. C. D., six inches by five inches (Fig. 124), and fold along dotted line X. X. so that A. B. falls on C. D. Fold points X. and X. along the dotted line so that they meet on centre line (Fig. 125) at point Y. You then have Fig. 126. Fold A. B. up on the two triangles X. and X. as far as the paper will go. Do the same with C. D. on the other side. You will then have Fig. 127. This is sometimes called a hat, but it is in an incomplete stage. Open out underneath between A. B. and C. D., as though to make a hat, but continue opening until the A. C. corner meets the D. B. corner. Press the paper flat. You then get Fig. 128. Now fold A. C. corner along the dotted lines

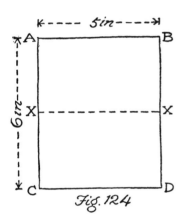

Fig. 124

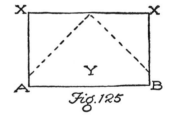

Fig. 125

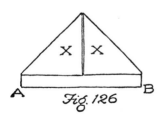

Fig. 126

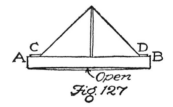

Open

Fig. 127

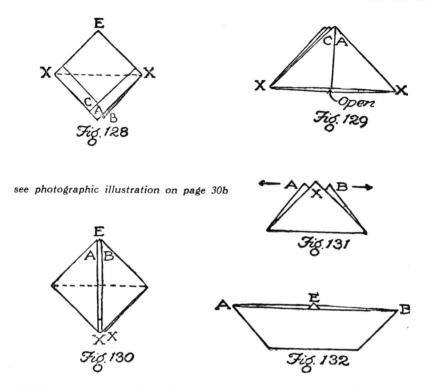

see photographic illustration on page 30b

Fig. 128

Fig. 129

Fig. 130

Fig. 131

Fig. 132

X. X. upon point E. Do the same on the other side with the corner B. D. You then have Fig. 129. This is the completed hat stage. Open out between X. and X. as before and bring these two points together once more flattening the paper (Fig. 130). Fold each point X. up on opposite sides so that they fall on E. covering points A. and B. on one side and C. D. on the other (Fig. 131). Now pull out A. C. and B. D. in opposite directions and you will have the boat (Fig. 132), point E. rising in the centre.

Note: If when folding up points C. A. and B. D. in Fig. 128, and the points X. X. in Fig. 130 you fold only to the dotted line instead of all the way to point E., the sides of the boat will come out much lower and point E. like a sail tip will come out much higher.

THE DART

Take two pieces of paper, one twice as long as wide, say 10 inches by 5 and the other 3 inches by 2. With the smaller piece fold as far as Fig. 126 in the boat, except that in this case you fold down one triangle on one side and the other on the reverse side. Then fold up the narrow strips at the bottom of the triangle as in the boat (Fig. 127), and tuck in the small projecting corners. Fold up corner G. along the dotted line and tuck G. into the opening at H. (Fig. 133). Do the same with point F., but on the other side. You will then have Fig. 134. This is the head of the dart. There will be an opening at the bottom at I.

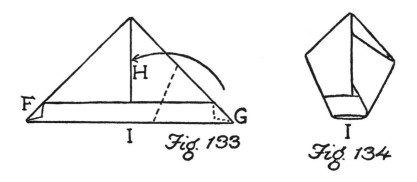

Fig. 133   *Fig. 134*

Now take the larger piece of paper and fold lengthwise down the centre. Open out and fold two of the end corners, A. and B. in so that they meet on the centre line (Fig. 135). With A. and B. folded, fold points C. and D. in over A. and B. so that they too meet on the centre line. You then get Fig. 136. Turn the paper over so that the back is up (Fig. 137). Fold points F. and E. on to the centre line (Fig. 138). Now fold the paper on the original crease from G. to H. and open points F. and E. away from each other, so that **F.** and **E.** lie flat on the table and the fold **G. H.** sticks up, **G. I.** and **G. J.** coming together. Turn the paper over. · **F.** and **E.** are points on the wings and **G. H.** makes the keel. Insert point **G.** into the head (Fig. 139) and you have the dart. Hold by the keel up near tip when about to throw. Turn the ends of the wings up very slightly at the corners. Much bigger darts may be made but the body part must be always proportional, e.g., twice as long as wide. The size and weight of the head will be found by experiment. The head may be also made of a large sheet of paper and converted into a hat.

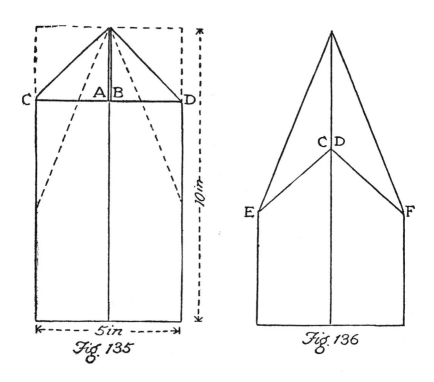

Fig. 135   *Fig. 136*

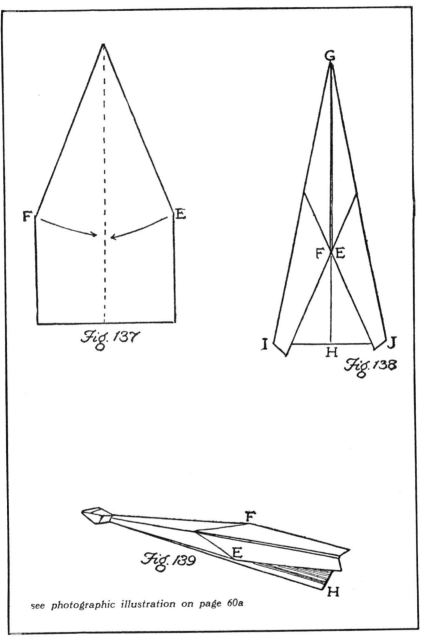

Fig. 137

Fig. 138

Fig. 139

see photographic illustration on page 60a

THE SECRET ENVELOPE

Take a square of paper, say 6 inches by 6 inches and fold it on each of its diagonals. Open out and then fold from one side one third of the way up, which in this case would be two inches. Fold down one third, or two inches, from the opposite side. Open out again and make similar folds from the other two sides, you will then have your paper creased as in Fig. 140. Now on each of the small squares marked X. make a sharp crease along the dotted lines. These creases must be upward whereas all the others are downward. Press in point 1 until it falls on point 5. This will bring down point 2 almost into place (Fig. 141). Close point 3 over on 6 (Fig. 142), and bring point 4 up behind 1, across the fold of 3 and over onto point 7. You will then have Fig. 143. Turn the paper over and finish the folding by bringing over the projecting points A. B. C. and D., folding one down on the other in order, B. folded on A., C. folded on B. (Fig. 144). Fold D. over C. and tuck its point in under A. The envelope made perfectly will look the same on both sides.

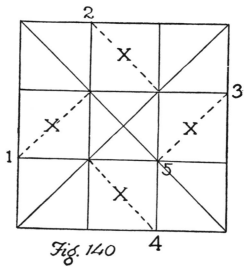

Fig. 140

46

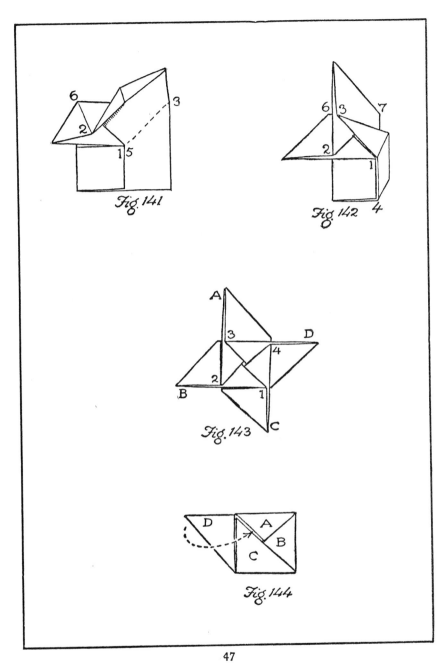

Fig. 141

Fig. 142

Fig. 143

Fig. 144

THE SUNFISH

Take a piece of paper twice as long as it is wide, say 8 inches by 4 inches. Fold it lengthwise along the centre, and as in Fig. 145, fold the corners so that they meet on the centre line A. meeting B., and C. meeting D. Fold the sides X. Y. over on each other so that X. falls on X. and Y. falls on Y. Turn the paper on one side and you will have Fig. 146. Hold the paper at each end near the points E. and F. and bend it upward as indicated by the arrows. This will cause the line E. F. to bend and the sides X. Y. and X.

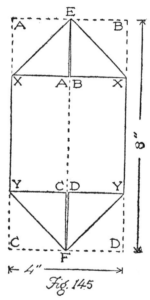

Fig. 145

Y. to separate from each other. Bring the points E. and F. all the way until they meet. Put point E. inside of point F. as shown in Fig. 147 but put the point E. all the way in. The sides F. Y. cover the sides E. X. Fig. 148 shows the back view. Holding E. and F. together push the bend H. I. at the point G. as far up as G. will go. This will bring the points H. and I. together and the side view of the paper will be somewhat as in Fig. 149. Now

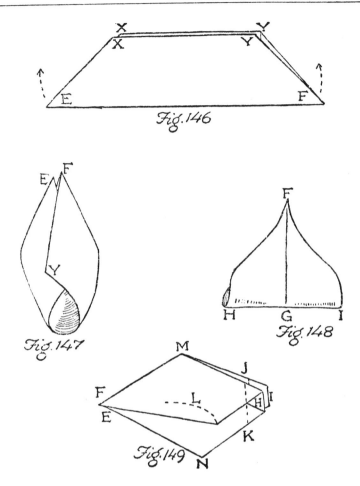

Fig. 146

Fig. 147

Fig. 148

Fig. 149

fold each of the ends H. and I. outward and in opposite directions from each other, along the dotted lines J. K. The folded ends should be at right angles to the rest of the paper. This is the tail of the fish. Tear, or better still, cut with scissors, along the dotted line L. and bend the cut piece out at right angles to the rest of the paper. This is one of the side fins. It will be found that the fin is a double piece of paper. Cut the inner part

49

along the right angle fold so that it may be opened down and spread out as shown in Fig. 150. Repeat on the other side. Close to F. make a circle with pen or pencil, and in the circle place a dot, this is one of the eyes. Repeat on the other side. Draw curved lines for the gills. Now by pulling the tail ends, **H.** and **I.** apart, the mouth of the fish is made to open. If a dorsal fin and

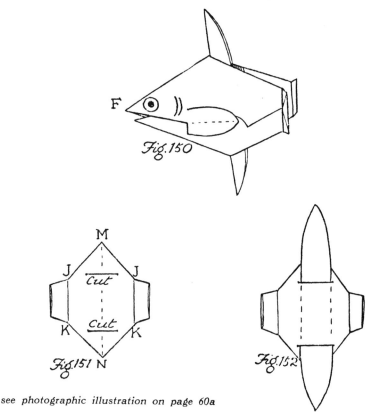

see photographic illustration on page 60a

an underneath fin be required open out the paper and cut two slits across the center fold as shown in Fig. 151. Take a narrow strip of paper, point each end and insert through slits as shown in Fig. 152.

THE TRUMPET

Take a six inch square of paper and fold along one diagonal. Then open out and proceed to roll the paper tightly around a pencil from one end of the diagonal crease to the other end, so that the diagonal rolls along itself as shown in Fig. 153. The pencil must be a round one and not one of those hexagonal or six sided pencils. When completely rolled it should look like Fig. 154. Push the pencil out and paste the last fold at A., or hold it in place with a rubber band. The ends of the roll will look like

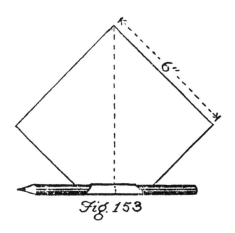

Fig. 153

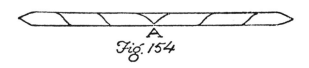

A

Fig. 154

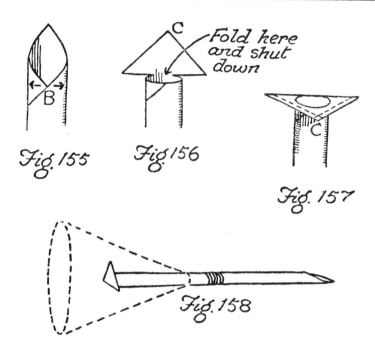

Fig. 155. Now from point marked B. at one end cut away on each side, in direction indicated by the small arrows, until the end piece may be opened out into a triangle shape (Fig. 156). The cuts must be at right angles to the main roll and are each a trifle over one third of the circumference of the rolled tube. Now fold the triangle piece at right angles to the tube so that it forms a little cover over the end (Fig. 157). Trim away a small part of the triangle on each side along the dotted lines indicated in sketch, but do not trim too close. Now place the other end of the tube in your mouth, and, instead of blowing, draw in your breath. This action will cause the little triangular paper lid to vibrate and the instrument will give a bleating sound. The noise can be made louder by rolling a cornucopia or horn and putting on the tube as shown in Fig. 158.

IV

Paper Tearing and Cutting

THE TREE

Roll a double-page spread of newspaper lengthwise to make a tube having a diameter of about an inch and a half. When about four inches from completing the roll insert a second double-page spread and continue rolling. In the same manner insert a third double-page spread and roll to complete the tube. Bend the tube in half and flatten one of the halves. Cut or tear down along the center of the flattened half (Fig. 159). Then flatten the torn pieces against each other so that the torn edges are at each side (Fig. 159 A). Tear down along the center of the pieces and you will have four groups of strips that will hang down around the unflattened lower half of the tube (Fig. 159 B). Hold the lower half with one hand and with a finger of the other hand in at top, carefully pull upward to start the tree growing. When started, work it up higher from the outside.

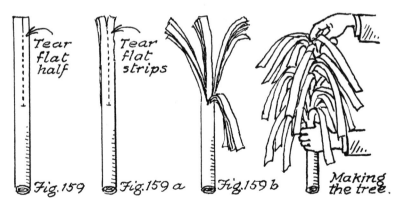

Tear flat half

Tear flat strips

Fig. 159   Fig. 159 a   Fig. 159 b   Making the tree.

THE LADDER

To make the ladder, the newspaper sheets are rolled as for the tree. Flatten the tube and then a third of the way from each end tear slightly over half way through the thickness of the roll and remove a section of the tube (Fig. 160). Make the tube ends round and bend them down as shown in Fig. 161.

With a finger in at the top of either of the ends, pull the paper up an inch or so and then pull up a bit at the other end. Continue to pull up alternately at each end until the paper will go no higher. The flat strips across the middle will form the steps of the ladder.

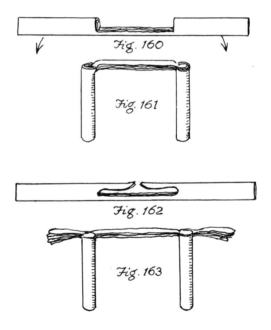

A variation of the ladder called "The Lattice" can be made by tearing the tube as shown in Fig. 162. Bend the ends down, the flaps outward, and bring the center strips up as when making the ladder.

THE MYSTERY LOOPS

Cut three strips of paper 20 inches, or more, long and 1 inch wide. Make them into three separate loops or rings completing each loop by pasting together the two ends of the strip. One strip is looped as the paper would naturally bend (Fig. 164.) The second strip however, before being looped is given a half turn or twist. This means that when pasted not only two opposite ends are joined but two opposite sides of the paper also come together (Fig. 165). The third strip is given a complete turn or twist and pasted (Fig. 166).

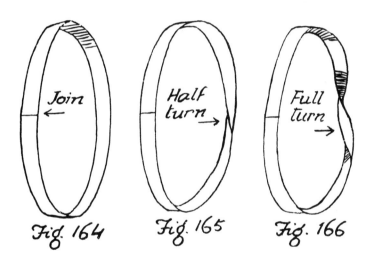

Fig. 164   *Fig. 165*   *Fig. 166*

Now when exhibiting the loops hold them so that the twisted parts are hidden in the hand. The first, or plain loop may be exhibited freely. With a scissors make an incision in the first loop and proceed to cut all along the center of the paper. When the cut is completed all the way around you will have two separate loops each one half inch wide (Fig. 167). Cut the other two loops along the centre in a similar manner and a strange thing will happen. The second loop instead of dividing into two loops will open out into one big loop (Fig. 168), while the third loop will become two loops but they will be linked together (Fig. 169.) The longer the original loops are, the less the twists will be noticed.

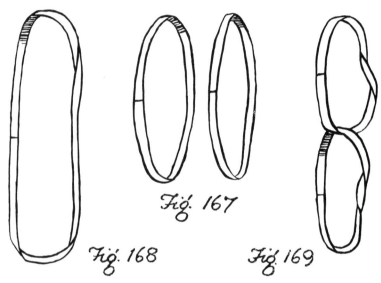

Fig. 167

Fig. 168

Fig. 169

When doing this loop-cutting stunt at a party it is better to cut the large loop (the loop with the half turn) last. A further surprise will be given if, when cutting the loop, you cut one third of the way in from either edge. As you cut along the strip you will come to where you started but it will be on the opposite side from where you are cutting. Pass by the starting place and continue cutting. You will again come to the starting place to end the cut. The large loop will open out but a small one will be linked with it. Make two halfturn loops, one for cutting to make Fig. 168 and the second to cut as just described. If you make a two inch wide strip you can by-pass the starting place several times and get a big surprise.

THE BIG HOLE IN THE SMALL
PIECE OF PAPER

A genuine hole large enough for a full-sized man to get through may be cut in a piece of paper 4 inches x 5 inches or of even smaller proportions. The size of the hole depends upon the fineness of the cutting. Fold across the centre of the paper so that the two four-inch ends coincide. You have then two rectangles back to back each measuring four inches by two and a half inches (Fig. 170). Keeping the paper folded tightly so that the cor-

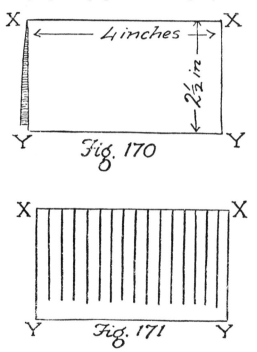

ners at the bottom coincide, cut with a sharp scissors, at intervals of one-fourth inch apart, from the folded line X. X. and through the double rectangles down to within one-fourth inch of the base line Y. Y. Be careful not to cut too close to the edge (Fig. 171).

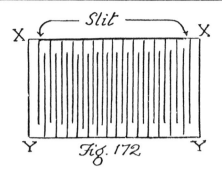

Fig. 172

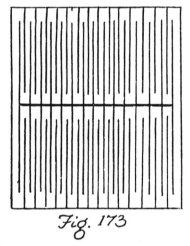

Fig. 173

Now holding the base lines together so that the cuts in both rectangles will remain in proper relation to each other, cut from the base lines Y. Y. up between each of the previous cuts (Fig. 172). Cut to within one-fourth inch of the X. X. fold. Do not cut up either of the end pieces of paper.

Now carefully slit along the fold from X. to X. leaving both end pieces of the fold intact. This may also be done by clipping off the extreme ends of all the centre folds. Fig. 173 shows the paper flattened out. It may now be opened in the centre and it will spread into a ring of considerable size.

THE PICNIC TABLE MAT

Take a circular piece of paper twelve inches or more in diameter. Fold it in half, then into quarters, then into eighths, then into sixteenths and into smaller divisions if so desired. The folds will all radiate from the centre and the folded paper will appear something like a closed fan (Fig. 174). Now tear or cut on either side of the fan-shaped piece of paper. The pieces cut out may be of any shape or pattern the only restriction being that the tear or cut must not go from one side to the other. Which ever side is torn the tear must go through all of the folds on that side. A mitred edged may be made. When opened out a symmetrical design appears.

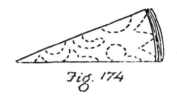

Fig. 174

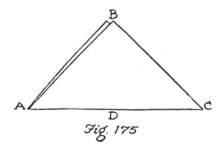

Fig. 175

THE FIVE-POINTED STAR

To make with one cut, or tear, a five-pointed star needs a special folding of the paper. First take a piece of paper about 5½ inches square and fold it on its diagonal so that two of its corners come together, as shown in Fig. 175, at B. Now comes the

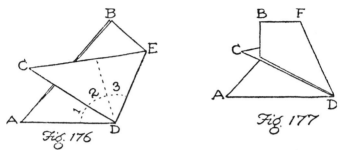

see photographic illustration on page 60a

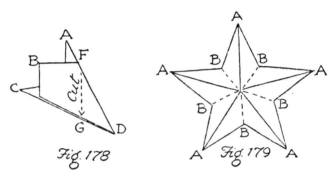

particular fold shown in Fig. 176. Point C. is folded from D. (which is directly in the centre of the baseline) across the edge A. B. in such a way that the angle C. D. E. is twice the angle A. D. C. The angle C. D. E. is two-thirds of the angle A. D. E., the remaining third being the angle A. D. C. Now fold along the dotted line so that the line D. E. falls on the line C. D. (Fig. 177) and when this is done fold the line A. D. back behind the paper along the line C. D. so that A. D. folds against the line F. D. This gives Fig. 178. Your paper is now ready for the tear or cut. It is better to cut the paper particularly for the making of the next object which needs straight edges. Cut from point F. along the dotted line to G. The line F. G. is parallel to B. E. and the point G. is half-way between E. and D. When opened out you have the star (Fig. 179).

Plate V The Dart (see page 43), The Sunfish (see page 48), and The Five-pointed Star (see page 59).

Plate VI The Baby Starling (see page 61), Bonbon Dish Number One (see page 75), and Bonbon Dish Number Three (see page 80).

THE BABY STARLING

Now comes a very pretty object. Born of a star, it is fitting that this object should be called the Baby Starling. First of all you will notice that some of the long radial lines from C. to A. are folded down and some are folded up. It is necessary that all of these five lines be folded up toward you and that the shorter lines from C. to B. be folded down. Bring all the C. B. lines together and, selecting the sharpest point A^1, keep it in the center,

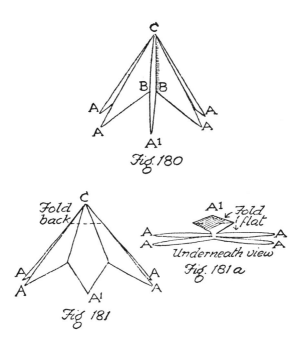

Fig. 180

Fig. 181

Fig. 181 a

folding the remaining four A. points together, two on each side as shown in Fig. 180.

Open point A^1 from underneath and flatten out as shown in Figs. 181 and 181a. Now fold back point C. behind the paper

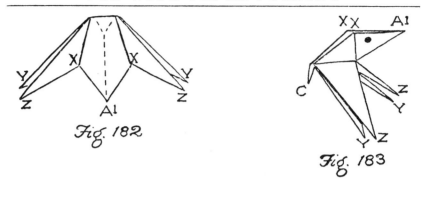

Fig. 182

Fig. 183

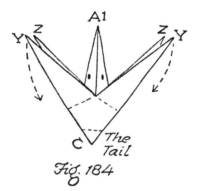

Fig. 184

along the dotted line which is about one-fifth of the way from
C. to A¹ (Fig. 182). Next fold the points X. and X. together
and the side view will be like Fig. 183. Make a small dot each
side of the fold. These dots are the bird's eyes. Now turn the
paper over and you will have Fig. 184. Take the first two points
Y. Y. and fold on the dotted lines; they will come down over
point C., but fold the tips back again so that they will fit inside of
the C. fold (Fig. 185). Now take the remaining two points and
in like manner fold them over and down. This gives Fig. 186.
Take these latter two pieces D. D. and tuck them under the previous folds E. E. as shown in Fig. 187. Now turn the paper over
again and you have the Baby Starling (Fig. 188). Pull his feet
out so that he may stand up.

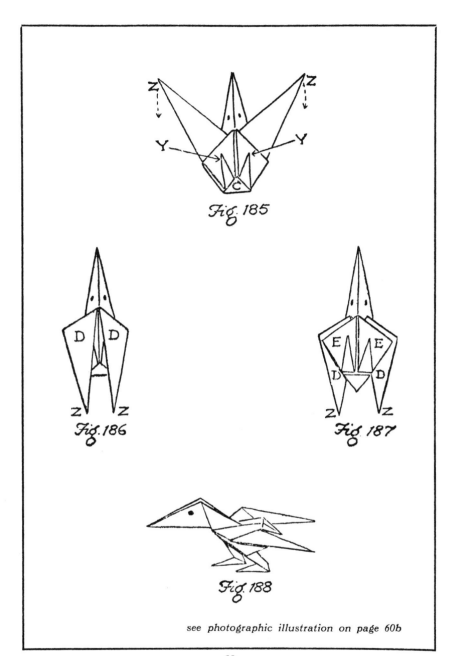

Fig. 185

Fig. 186

Fig. 187

Fig. 188

see *photographic illustration on page 60b*

THE AVIATOR'S HELMET

Take a piece of paper 5 inches by 6 inches and fold in halves so that you have two rectangles measuring 5 inches by 3 inches as shown in Fig. 189. Now fold B. D. over on A. C. to get the centre line marked (Figs. 190 and 190a). Fold points A. and B. down to meet on this centre line (Fig. 191). Next, as in making the old-fashioned hat, fold up the strip C. D. on the points A. B. This strip will be about one-half inch wide. There will be another strip on the other side which you will fold back (Fig. 191). Bring back points A. and B. to their original positions. You will then have Fig. 192. Now with the strip folded, bring up D. on E., as shown in Fig. 193. Bring in the same manner C. on E. (Fig. 194). Next fold D. B. along the dotted line so that

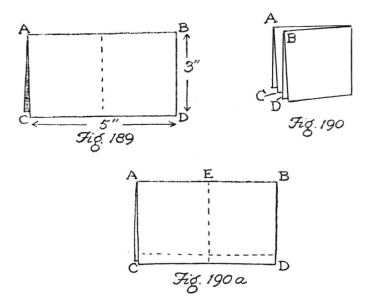

Fig. 189

Fig. 190

Fig. 190 a

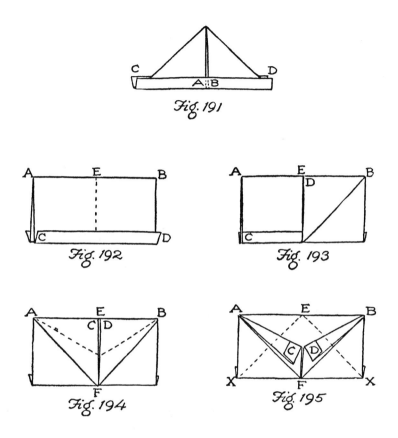

Fig. 191

Fig. 192   Fig. 193

Fig. 194   Fig. 195

D. B. falls on F. B.   Do the same with C. A. so that it falls on
F. A. (Fig. 195).   Fold points A. and B. back along the dotted
lines E. X. and tuck them in behind the folded strip.   Fig. 196
shows the back view.   Fig. 197 is the front.   Lift up point F.
and fold it under C. and D. along the dotted line.   Open out

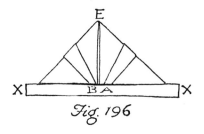

Fig. 196

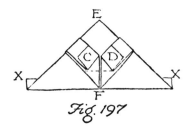

Fig. 197

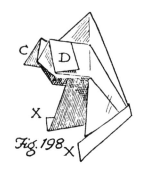

Fig. 198

under D. and C., and you have the helmet (Fig. 198). The back band **X. X.** may be bent around in front, one end of it being tucked into the other. This is the strap that fastens under the aviator's chin.

THE CRADLE

Fold a square of paper—as shown at the beginning of the book
—to Fig. 3a. This is Fig. 199. Fold along the diagonal L. J.
so that points M. and K. come together as shown in Fig.
200. Points B. and D. will be folded in between. Pull out
point B., as shown in Fig. 201, and point D., as shown in Fig.
202. Now fold point G. up along the line M. J. until G. rests
on B. (Fig. 203). Do the same with point H. bringing it to D.

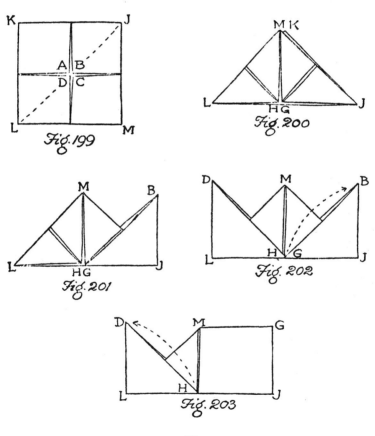

Fig. 199

Fig. 200

Fig. 201

Fig. 202

Fig. 203

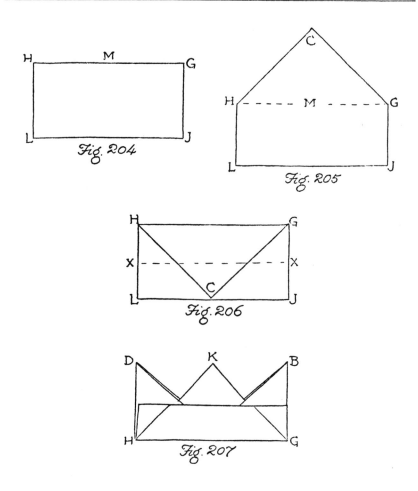

Fig. 204

Fig. 205

Fig. 206

Fig. 207

You will now have Fig. 204. Point C. will be found in behind this rectangle. Pull it out as shown in Fig. 205. Fold point C. down on the outside until C. rests on the line L. J. (Fig. 206). Now fold the line H. G. along the dotted line X. X. so that it lies along the line L. J. and covers the point C. This brings you to Fig. 207. Repeat all of these folds on the other side bringing

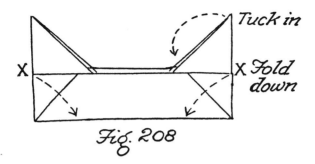

Fig. 208

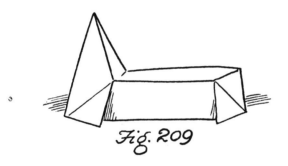

Fig. 209

I. on D., and bringing F. on C., pulling out A. and folding it under in the same way that you folded C. You will now find four little triangles, two on each side, X. and X.; fold these down in the direction indicated by the arrows (Fig. 208). Then turn point B. in and fold down and you will have the cradle (Fig. 209).

69

ANOTHER DOUBLE BOAT

Taking a square of paper fold the corners A. B. C. and D. into the centre (Fig. 210).   Fold back the corners I. and G. along the dotted lines so that I. and G. meet.   This gives you Fig. 211. Now fold the points F. and H. to meet on top of the corners A.

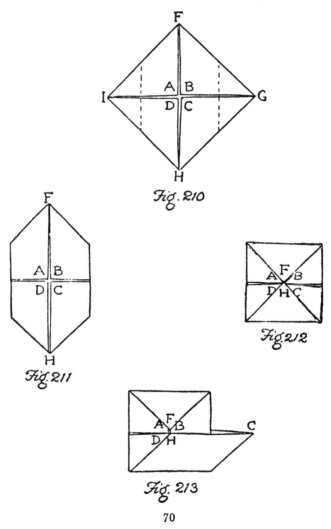

Fig. 210

Fig. 211

Fig. 212

Fig. 213

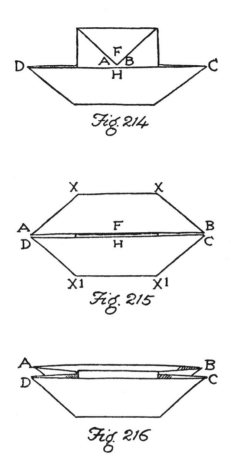

Fig. 214

Fig. 215

Fig. 216

B. C. and D. in the centre (Fig. 212). Pull out the corner C., as shown in Fig. 213; then D., as shown in Fig. 214. Treat A. and B. in the same manner. You now have Fig. 215. Fold X. X. back along the line that runs between F. and H. so that X. and X. rests on X^1 and X^1. This is the double boat (Fig. 216).

71

THE LAMPSHADE

Fold a square of paper as shown in the second manner of folding, that is along the two diagonals and across the centre parallel to the sides (Fig. 217). The folds from F. to H. and from
I. to G. are drawn in solid lines, which is to indicate that they
are raised toward you. The dotted diagonal lines are depressed,
which means that the raised edges of their folds are on the reverse side of the paper. Fold in the points A. B. C. and D. to
the centre E. (Fig. 218). Now fold the triangle I. F. G. back
along its base line I. G. so that point F. coincides with point H.
This gives Fig. 219. Fold the point G. along the dotted line
down on point L. which is half-way between G. and H. (Fig. 220).
Now take up point G. and fold it down again to L., but this time
on the back (Fig. 221). Repeat with point I. folding it both
ways to M. (Fig. 222). These folds are only to get the creases.
Now open the paper out again to Fig. 218 and fold it back diagonally once more, but this time from F. to H. bringing points I.
and G. together (Fig. 223). Fold the corners F. and H. for

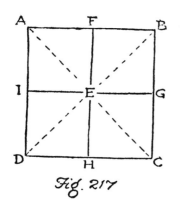

Fig. 217

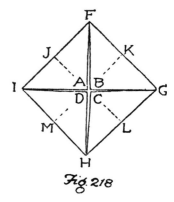

Fig. 218

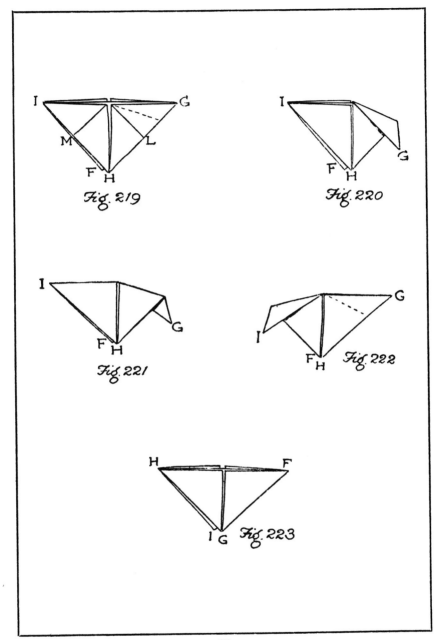

Fig. 219

Fig. 220

Fig. 221

Fig. 222

Fig. 223

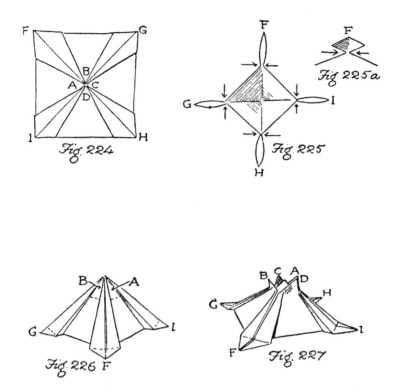

creases as you folded G. and I. The paper, when opened out and viewed from the top, will look like Fig. 224. Turn the paper over and squeeze the points together as indicated by the arrows (Fig. 225). Open one of the corners F. and flatten it down as shown in Fig. 225a. Repeat with the other three corners and you will have an object like Fig. 226. Take out the corners A. B. C. and D. at the top and crease them back a little way from the top as indicated by the dotted lines. Fold back the corners F. G. H. and I. and you have the Lampshade (Fig. 227).

FOUR BONBON DISHES

Dish Number 1

Take a square of paper and first crease it on both diagonals. Then fold the corners A. B. C. D. to the centre (Fig. 228). Turn the paper over and fold the new corners F. G. H. and I. to the centre (Fig. 299). Having done this to get the creases, open the paper back to Fig. 228. Now squeeze the corners F. G. H. and I. to meet together in the centre so as to leave the points A. B. C. and D. sticking up (Fig. 230).

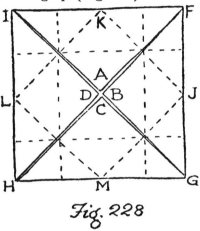

Fig. 228

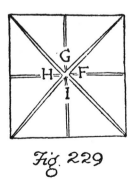

Fig. 229

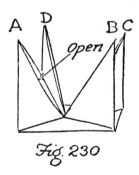

Fig. 230

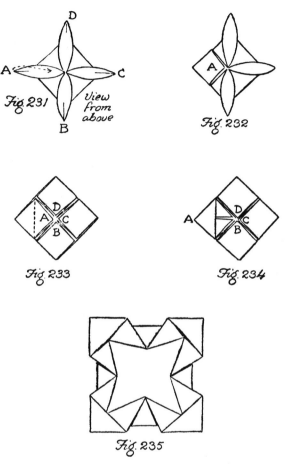

see *photographic illustration on page 60b*

Holding F. G. H. and I. in the centre, open out A. and flatten
the point down in the centre as shown in Fig. 232. Repeat with
B. C. and D. and you have Fig. 233. Fold back point A. along
the dotted line (Fig. 234). Repeat with B. C. and D. Open
out the corners and you have the dish (Fig. 235).

76

Dish Number 2

Commence as with Dish Number 1 folding the corners A. B. C. and D. to the centre, turning the paper over and folding F. G. H. and I. to the reverse centre (Fig. 236). Fold the next corners J. K. L. and M. back on A. B. C. and D. This gives you Fig. 237. Keeping the reverse side of the paper uppermost, open it out to Fig. 238, leaving A. B. C. and D. folded underneath. Now crease the paper on the dotted lines. This is done

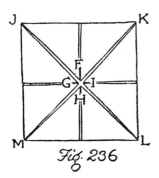

Fig. 236

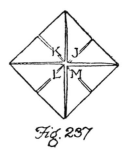

Fig. 237

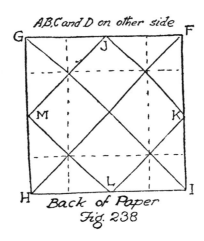

Fig. 238

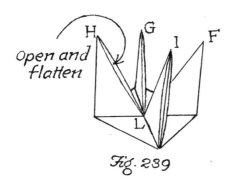

Fig. 239

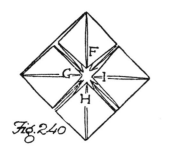

Fig. 240

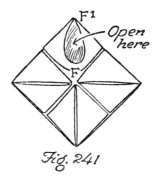

Fig. 241

by folding each of the four sides to the centre. Open the paper
out again and then squeeze the points J. K. L. and M. to meet
in the centre, leaving F. G. H. and I. standing up (Fig. 239).
Holding the points J. K. L. and M. together in the centre, open
out and flatten down the points F. G. H. and I. in the centre to
make Fig. 240. You have now four little squares, each one with

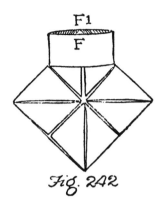

Fig. 242

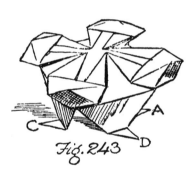

Fig. 243

a diagonal opening. Open out this diagonal and flatten the paper back so that it forms a rectangle. Fig. 241 shows F. being opened. Point F. folds over on F¹ (Fig. 242). Do the same with each of the other three squares. The paper is then opened out slightly and the points A. B. C. and D. brought down from underneath giving each of these points a small fold to make the feet of the dish (Fig. 243).

Dish Number 3

Fold a square of paper in the second manner of folding as described earlier in the book. This is Fig. 244 folded on both diagonals and parallel to the sides, the folds F. H. and G. I. being uppermost, the diagonal folds being depressed. Bring the points A. B. C. and D. together at the bottom, the centre point E. sticking up at the top. This leaves F. G. H. and I. pointing out at the sides (Fig. 245). Fold up the point C. to E. along the dotted line H. G. (Fig. 246). In like manner fold up the points A. B. and D. creasing each triangle up the centre as it is folded. This brings you to Fig. 247, the underside view of which is Fig. 247a. Holding closely together, the points indicated by arrows

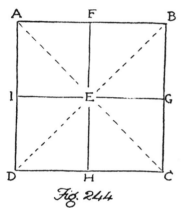

Fig. 244

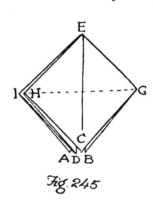

Fig. 245

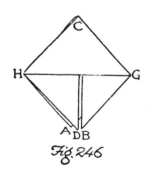

Fig. 246

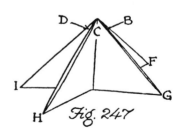

Fig. 247

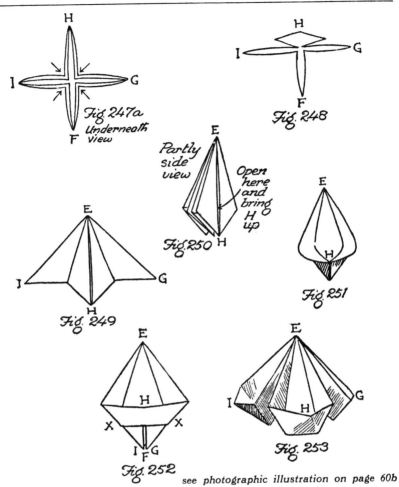

Fig. 247a
Underneath view

Fig. 248

Partly side view

Open here and bring H up

Fig. 250

Fig. 251

Fig. 249

Fig. 252

Fig. 253

see photographic illustration on page 60b

open out one of the folds H. and flatten it down as shown in Fig. 248. This makes Fig. 249. Do the same with F. G. and I. and the paper will look like Fig. 250. Now press point H. upward so as to open the space from H. to E. (Fig. 251). Fold back point H. along the line X. X. so that H. rests on the centre line from E. (Fig. 252). Do the same with F. G. and I. and you have Fig. 253, which is Dish Number 3.

81

Dish Number 4

Fold the paper as in Dish Number 2 to Fig. 236. This is now Fig. 254. Squeeze together the lines F. X., G. X., H. X. and I. X. so that the points X. X. X. X. meet at the bottom, F. G. H. and I. coming to the top leaving points J. K. L. and M. sticking out. Fig. 255 shows the points X. X. X. X. being squeezed in, and Fig. 256 shows underneath view. Now flatten the paper so as to have one of the triangles M. H. L. toward you. Now

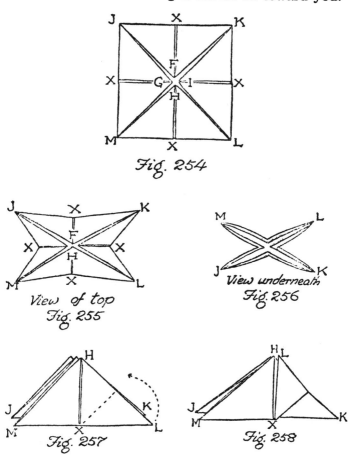

Fig. 254

View of top
Fig. 255

View underneath
Fig. 256

Fig. 257

Fig. 258

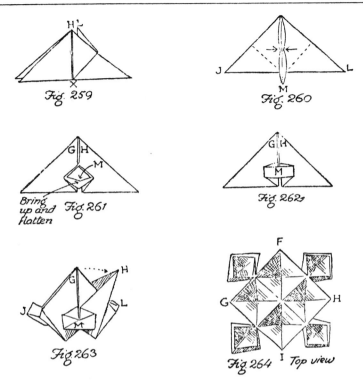

Fig. 259

Fig. 260

Bring up and flatten   Fig. 261

Fig. 262

Fig 263

Fig 264   Top view

bend up point L. so that it folds on point H. (Fig. 258). Bring point L. down again and fold it up once more, but this time at the back of the triangle (Fig. 259). Crease the fold hard each time. This is just to get the creases. Do the same with points J. K. and M. The paper will now stand up like Fig. 260. Holding at the creased point indicated by the arrows above M., press the point M. back and you will have a little square with a diagonal opening (Fig. 261). Squeeze the upper and lower part of this diagonal opening together so that the diagonal will open and fold out as shown in Fig. 262. Do the same with the points J. K. and L. Now pull out from the top the points F. G. H. and I. Fig. 263 shows H. pulled out. When all points are out you have a very pretty little bonbon dish. Fig. 264 shows the view from the top.

THE JAPANESE LANTERN

Fold a square of paper as described in the second method of folding, that is across the centre parallel to the side and along both diagonals. Fig. 265 shows the folds, the diagonal folds being up toward you while the lines from F. to H. and from I. to G. are depressed. Fold the paper so that I. and G. meet together underneath, leaving E. pointing up and A. D. coming together on one side while B. and C. coincide on the other (Fig. 266). Fold H. C. so that the point C. falls on E. (Fig. 267). Do the same with D. (Fig. 268). Fold in like manner up on the back points A. and B. You will now have Fig. 269 with points J. K. L. and M. sticking out around the sides. Take point J. and fold it over along the dotted line so that J. E. coincides with H. E. Crease the line hard (Fig. 270). Now open J. back and once more fold it over on the line H. E., but this time it is the line H. J. which falls on H. E. The point J. being up toward E. Again crease hard (Fig. 271). Open out J. once more and you will find two creased lines forming an X. (Fig. 272). Squeeze

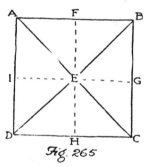

Fig. 265

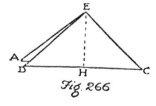

Fig. 266

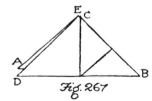

Fig. 267

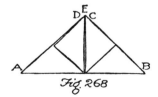

Fig. 268

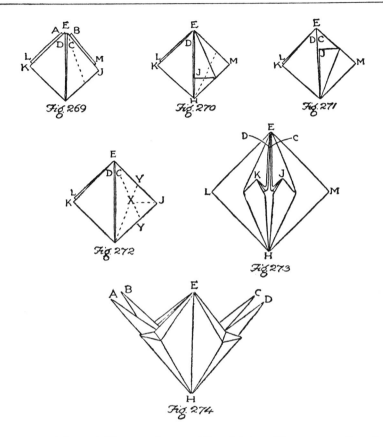

the points Y. and Y. together at X. which will crease a line from
X. to J. and leave point J. sticking up.   Fold point J. up in the
direction of point E. at the top.   Do the same with K. and you
will get Fig. 273.   Repeat on the other side with L. and M.   Up
at point E. on the J. K. side will be found the points D. and C.
hidden behind the folds of the paper.   Pull them out as shown
in Fig. 274 which gives a side view.   Points A. and B. will likewise be hidden and are also to be pulled out.   Holding C. D. on
one side and B. A. on the other blow into a small hole which will
be found at H.   The result is the Japanese Lantern.

V

How Charlie Bought His Boat

A PAPER FOLDING STORY

(This story is told by making the objects mentioned in the illustrations under the first method of creasing and folding the paper, as the story proceeds, using the one piece of paper and changing it from one thing to the next until the last boat is made, the Chinese Junk (Fig. 35). Here the story is given in

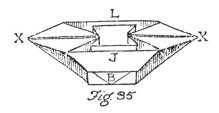

Fig. 35

outline. It presupposes ability to make the various objects. Details can be added in the telling.)

Charlie had lived in the city with his father and mother but now they had moved into the country. Near the house they found a small lake or pond. One day Charlie said, "Mother, can't I have a rowboat on the pond?" "Why, I think you might; but we'll ask father when he comes home, and see what he says." So that night they talked it over and finally father said, "Yes, you can have a boat, if you will be real careful." He gave Charlie some money, and told him to take the trolley and go into the village, where he would see a sign, "Boats for Sale."

By and by Charlie reached the village, and as he was walking down the street, he kept looking in the windows as boys do.

He came to a window of a store where they sold silver things, and as he looked he said to himself, "There's something I think mother would like to have." So he went in and pointed to it and asked the man what it was. The man took it out of the window and put it on the counter and said, "Why, that is a salt cellar, with a place for salt, pepper, sugar and mustard." (Fig. 5.) (Here the story teller puts the object on his hand and shows it, and he does the same with each of the others as they are made.)

"I'll take it," Charlie said. So the man wrapped it up and Charlie paid for it and started on.

He hadn't gone very far before he came to another store where there were more silver things. And in the window he saw something he thought his mother would rather have than the salt cellar. So he went in and pointing to it said to the

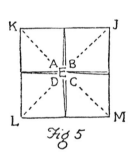

Fig 5

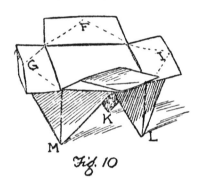

Fig. 10

man, "Would you give me that for this salt cellar?" The man said, "You mean this cake basket?" (Fig 10) putting it on the counter. "Yes," Charlie said. "Why, yes," the man said, so Charlie gave him the salt cellar and he wrapped up the cake basket and gave it to Charlie.

But pretty soon Charlie began to think, "I don't believe mother would care for this cake basket," and just then he happened to be in front of a store where they sold things for ladies.

"I guess I'll see if they won't give me for this cake basket something for mother to wear," he said to himself. When he asked the man in the store if he would do this, the man said, "Why yes, I'll give you one of these and some money too, because the cake basket is worth more than this." And he held up this shirt waist (Fig. 12).

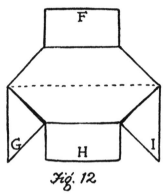

Fig. 12

And now that he had something for his mother he felt he ought to get something for his father; and inasmuch as he had something for his mother to wear, he said, "I'll buy something for father to wear," so he went into a tailor's store and bought a pair of trousers (Fig. 13).

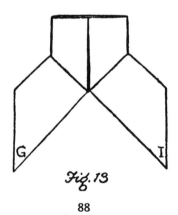

Fig. 13

Charlie had almost forgotten what he came to the city for, when suddenly he saw a sign BOATS FOR SALE. "That's the place I'm looking for," he said and went in. When he told the man what he wanted the man said "Yes, we have boats for sale; come out in the yard and see them." But then Charlie found they were motor-boats, each with two funnels, and he had to say, "I don't want a motor-boat, I want a rowboat." "All right," said the man, "down the street a little way you'll find another place, maybe you can get a rowboat." So along the street he went.

He began to think maybe his father and mother would like to buy their own clothes, and just then he found himself in front of a furniture store. And there in the window he saw something he liked, so he went in and said to the man, "Would you give me that table for these trousers and shirt waist?" "Why yes;" the the man said, "I'd be glad to." So Charlie started off carrying the table (Fig. 17).

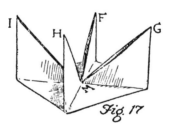

Fig. 17

By this time he had walked a good deal and he was thirsty and while he was wondering where he could get a drink of water, he spied a windmill (Fig. 18) and he knew there would be water where there was a windmill so he went over and got a drink of water.

And now at last he saw that sign BOATS FOR SALE, so into the store he went. "I'm looking for a rowboat," Charlie said. "Well," the man said, "I have some rowboats, but they

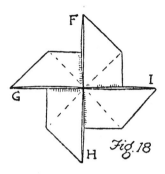

F
G
I
H *Fig. 18*

are all twin boats." (Fig. 19). "What in the world could I do with boats like that," Charlie said, and walked out. "Well," the man said, "go down to the next corner, and turn to the right; you'll see a place where they sell boats. Maybe that man has rowboats."

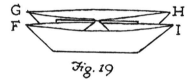

G H
F I
Fig. 19

So along Charlie went, carrying the table. Soon he came to the store and when he asked the man if he had boats for sale, the man said, "Why yes, we've got boats for sale. Take a look at them;

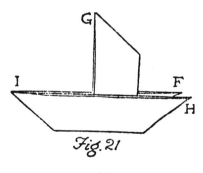

G
I F
H
Fig. 21

they're in the yard here." But when Charlie saw them he said, "Why, they're all sailboats." (Fig 21). "I want a rowboat." So he could buy none there.

By this time the table began to feel heavy and he wondered why he had bought it anyway. "Mother has plenty of furniture," he said. Just then he came to an open space and looking over into the field he spied some chickens. "There," he said, "We haven't a single chicken on our place. Couldn't I trade this table for one." He spoke to the farmer and the farmer said, "Why, yes; how would you like to give me your table for this rooster." (Fig. 23.). That was just what Charlie wanted, so he gave the farmer the table and put the rooster under his arm and started on.

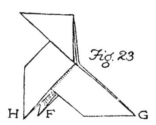

He'd gone a good ways by this time, and it suddenly occurred to him that he hadn't been doing what he was sent to do—buy a rowboat, and this made him feel rather uncomfortable. He counted his money and he felt quite sure he didn't have enough left to buy a boat. While he was wondering what he should do a sudden gale of wind blew his hat off, and when he raised his hand to catch it, the rooster got away! There he was with so much money spent and nothing to show for it, and his hat gone! And so he walked along, thinking very hard, looking down at the ground. All of a sudden he spied something and stooped over and grabbed it. It was a pocketbook with some money in this

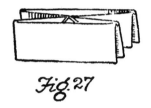

Fig. 27

side and some in this (Fig. 27). By this time he was pretty well out of the city, he did not see any one to speak to, there was no house right there, so he said, "Well, I'll use this money now to buy a boat, and when I get home we'll try to find the owner of this pocketbook and send the same amount of money back to him."

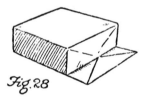

Fig. 28

"But first, I must get a hat. I can't go home this way," he said to himself. So he hunted up a store and bought this cap. (Fig. 28).

Then he thought, "I really ought to take something home to Mother." The only thing he saw that didn't cost too much was this picture frame. He thought it would be nice for mother to put father's picture in (Fig. 32).

By this time the day was nearly gone and he said, "I'll buy any kind of a boat now, I don't care what it's like. The next place I find where they sell boats, I'll buy one of them." So he kept looking for a sign, until after a little while he saw one,

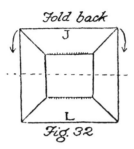

Fold back

Fig. 32

BOATS FOR SALE. In he went and asked the man, "Can you sell me a boat?" "Yes," the man said, "but I've got the queerest looking boats you ever saw." "Never mind," Charlie said, "I been looking so long, I'll take any kind of a boat. Let me see them." "Here they are," the man said and when Charlie asked him what they were he said "We call them Chinese junks."

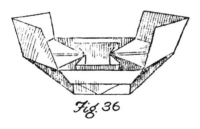

Fig. 36

(Fig. 36). "All right," Charlie said, "here's your money; send that boat to my father," and he told the man where they lived. So after all his trouble Charlie got a boat at last and went home happy.

93

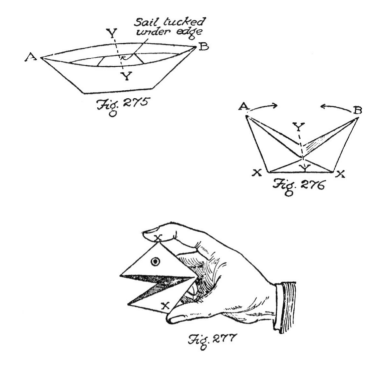

Fig. 275

Fig. 276

Fig. 277

THE GOOSE'S HEAD

And now, boys and girls, don't forget to pick up any little bits of paper that may have fallen on the floor. To help you pick them up you need a goose's head, and you make it this way. First make the old-fashioned boat as shown (Fig. 132), page 42. Then tuck the sail in under one of the edges as shown (Fig. 275). Now bend the boat across the middle along the dotted line Y. Y., and the points A. and B. will come together (Fig. 276). Hold the paper between fingers and thumb at the points X. X. (Fig. 277). Put in dots for eyes. This is the goose's head and it will help you considerably in picking up.

THE END

A CATALOG OF SELECTED DOVER
BOOKS IN ALL FIELDS OF INTEREST

DRAWINGS OF REMBRANDT, edited by Seymour Slive. Updated Lippmann, Hofstede de Groot edition, with definitive scholarly apparatus. All portraits, biblical sketches, landscapes, nudes. Oriental figures, classical studies, together with selection of work by followers. 550 illustrations. Total of 630pp. 9⅛ × 12¼.
21485-0, 21486-9 Pa., Two-vol. set $29.90

GHOST AND HORROR STORIES OF AMBROSE BIERCE, Ambrose Bierce. 24 tales vividly imagined, strangely prophetic, and decades ahead of their time in technical skill: "The Damned Thing," "An Inhabitant of Carcosa," "The Eyes of the Panther," "Moxon's Master," and 20 more. 199pp. 5⅜ × 8½.   20767-6 Pa. $4.95

ETHICAL WRITINGS OF MAIMONIDES, Maimonides. Most significant ethical works of great medieval sage, newly translated for utmost precision, readability. Laws Concerning Character Traits, Eight Chapters, more. 192pp. 5⅜ × 8½.
24522-5 Pa. $4.50

THE EXPLORATION OF THE COLORADO RIVER AND ITS CANYONS, J. W. Powell. Full text of Powell's 1,000-mile expedition down the fabled Colorado in 1869. Superb account of terrain, geology, vegetation, Indians, famine, mutiny, treacherous rapids, mighty canyons, during exploration of last unknown part of continental U.S. 400pp. 5⅜ × 8½.   20094-9 Pa. $7.95

HISTORY OF PHILOSOPHY, Julián Marías. Clearest one-volume history on the market. Every major philosopher and dozens of others, to Existentialism and later. 505pp. 5⅜ × 8½.   21739-6 Pa. $9.95

ALL ABOUT LIGHTNING, Martin A. Uman. Highly readable non-technical survey of nature and causes of lightning, thunderstorms, ball lightning, St. Elmo's Fire, much more. Illustrated. 192pp. 5⅜ × 8½.   25237-X Pa. $5.95

SAILING ALONE AROUND THE WORLD, Captain Joshua Slocum. First man to sail around the world, alone, in small boat. One of great feats of seamanship told in delightful manner. 67 illustrations. 294pp. 5⅜ × 8½.   20326-3 Pa. $4.95

LETTERS AND NOTES ON THE MANNERS, CUSTOMS AND CONDITIONS OF THE NORTH AMERICAN INDIANS, George Catlin. Classic account of life among Plains Indians: ceremonies, hunt, warfare, etc. 312 plates. 572pp. of text. 6⅛ × 9¼.   22118-0, 22119-9, Pa. Two-vol. set $17.90

ALASKA: The Harriman Expedition, 1899, John Burroughs, John Muir, et al. Informative, engrossing accounts of two-month, 9,000-mile expedition. Native peoples, wildlife, forests, geography, salmon industry, glaciers, more. Profusely illustrated. 240 black-and-white line drawings. 124 black-and-white photographs. 3 maps. Index. 576pp. 5⅜ × 8½.   25109-8 Pa. $11.95

THE BOOK OF BEASTS: Being a Translation from a Latin Bestiary of the Twelfth Century, T. H. White. Wonderful catalog real and fanciful beasts: manticore, griffin, phoenix, amphivius, jaculus, many more. White's witty erudite commentary on scientific, historical aspects. Fascinating glimpse of medieval mind. Illustrated. 296pp. 5⅜ × 8¼. (Available in U.S. only) 24609-4 Pa. $6.95

FRANK LLOYD WRIGHT: ARCHITECTURE AND NATURE With 160 Illustrations, Donald Hoffmann. Profusely illustrated study of influence of nature—especially prairie—on Wright's designs for Fallingwater, Robie House, Guggenheim Museum, other masterpieces. 96pp. 9¼ × 10¾. 25098-9 Pa. $8.95

FRANK LLOYD WRIGHT'S FALLINGWATER, Donald Hoffmann. Wright's famous waterfall house: planning and construction of organic idea. History of site, owners, Wright's personal involvement. Photographs of various stages of building. Preface by Edgar Kaufmann, Jr. 100 illustrations. 112pp. 9¼ × 10. 23671-4 Pa. $8.95

YEARS WITH FRANK LLOYD WRIGHT: Apprentice to Genius, Edgar Tafel. Insightful memoir by a former apprentice presents a revealing portrait of Wright the man, the inspired teacher, the greatest American architect. 372 black-and-white illustrations. Preface. Index. vi + 228pp. 8¼ × 11. 24801-1 Pa. $10.95

THE STORY OF KING ARTHUR AND HIS KNIGHTS, Howard Pyle. Enchanting version of King Arthur fable has delighted generations with imaginative narratives of exciting adventures and unforgettable illustrations by the author. 41 illustrations. xviii + 313pp. 6⅛ × 9¼. 21445-1 Pa. $6.95

THE GODS OF THE EGYPTIANS, E. A. Wallis Budge. Thorough coverage of numerous gods of ancient Egypt by foremost Egyptologist. Information on evolution of cults, rites and gods; the cult of Osiris; the Book of the Dead and its rites; the sacred animals and birds; Heaven and Hell; and more. 956pp. 6⅛ × 9¼. 22055-9, 22056-7 Pa., Two-vol. set $21.90

A THEOLOGICO-POLITICAL TREATISE, Benedict Spinoza. Also contains unfinished *Political Treatise*. Great classic on religious liberty, theory of government on common consent. R. Elwes translation. Total of 421pp. 5⅜ × 8½. 20249-6 Pa. $7.95

INCIDENTS OF TRAVEL IN CENTRAL AMERICA, CHIAPAS, AND YUCATAN, John L. Stephens. Almost single-handed discovery of Maya culture; exploration of ruined cities, monuments, temples; customs of Indians. 115 drawings. 892pp. 5⅜ × 8½. 22404-X, 22405-8 Pa., Two-vol. set $15.90

LOS CAPRICHOS, Francisco Goya. 80 plates of wild, grotesque monsters and caricatures. Prado manuscript included. 183pp. 6⅛ × 9⅜. 22384-1 Pa. $5.95

AUTOBIOGRAPHY: The Story of My Experiments with Truth, Mohandas K. Gandhi. Not hagiography, but Gandhi in his own words. Boyhood, legal studies, purification, the growth of the Satyagraha (nonviolent protest) movement. Critical, inspiring work of the man who freed India. 480pp. 5⅜ × 8½. (Available in U.S. only) 24593-4 Pa. $6.95

ILLUSTRATED DICTIONARY OF HISTORIC ARCHITECTURE, edited by Cyril M. Harris. Extraordinary compendium of clear, concise definitions for over 5,000 important architectural terms complemented by over 2,000 line drawings. Covers full spectrum of architecture from ancient ruins to 20th-century Modernism. Preface. 592pp. 7½ × 9⅜. 24444-X Pa. $15.95

THE NIGHT BEFORE CHRISTMAS, Clement Moore. Full text, and woodcuts from original 1848 book. Also critical, historical material. 19 illustrations. 40pp. 4⅝ × 6. 22797-9 Pa. $2.50

THE LESSON OF JAPANESE ARCHITECTURE: 165 Photographs, Jiro Harada. Memorable gallery of 165 photographs taken in the 1930's of exquisite Japanese homes of the well-to-do and historic buildings. 13 line diagrams. 192pp. 8⅜ × 11¼. 24778-3 Pa. $10.95

THE AUTOBIOGRAPHY OF CHARLES DARWIN AND SELECTED LETTERS, edited by Francis Darwin. The fascinating life of eccentric genius composed of an intimate memoir by Darwin (intended for his children); commentary by his son, Francis; hundreds of fragments from notebooks, journals, papers; and letters to and from Lyell, Hooker, Huxley, Wallace and Henslow. xi + 365pp. 5⅜ × 8. 20479-0 Pa. $6.95

WONDERS OF THE SKY: Observing Rainbows, Comets, Eclipses, the Stars and Other Phenomena, Fred Schaaf. Charming, easy-to-read poetic guide to all manner of celestial events visible to the naked eye. Mock suns, glories, Belt of Venus, more. Illustrated. 299pp. 5¼ × 8¼. 24402-4 Pa. $7.95

BURNHAM'S CELESTIAL HANDBOOK, Robert Burnham, Jr. Thorough guide to the stars beyond our solar system. Exhaustive treatment. Alphabetical by constellation: Andromeda to Cetus in Vol. 1; Chamaeleon to Orion in Vol. 2; and Pavo to Vulpecula in Vol. 3. Hundreds of illustrations. Index in Vol. 3. 2,000pp. 6⅛ × 9¼. 23567-X, 23568-8, 23673-0 Pa., Three-vol. set $41.85

STAR NAMES: Their Lore and Meaning, Richard Hinckley Allen. Fascinating history of names various cultures have given to constellations and literary and folkloristic uses that have been made of stars. Indexes to subjects. Arabic and Greek names. Biblical references. Bibliography. 563pp. 5⅜ × 8½. 21079-0 Pa. $8.95

THIRTY YEARS THAT SHOOK PHYSICS: The Story of Quantum Theory, George Gamow. Lucid, accessible introduction to influential theory of energy and matter. Careful explanations of Dirac's anti-particles, Bohr's model of the atom, much more. 12 plates. Numerous drawings. 240pp. 5⅜ × 8½. 24895-X Pa. $5.95

CHINESE DOMESTIC FURNITURE IN PHOTOGRAPHS AND MEASURED DRAWINGS, Gustav Ecke. A rare volume, now affordably priced for antique collectors, furniture buffs and art historians. Detailed review of styles ranging from early Shang to late Ming. Unabridged republication. 161 black-and-white drawings, photos. Total of 224pp. 8⅜ × 11¼. (Available in U.S. only) 25171-3 Pa. $13.95

VINCENT VAN GOGH: A Biography, Julius Meier-Graefe. Dynamic, penetrating study of artist's life, relationship with brother, Theo, painting techniques, travels, more. Readable, engrossing. 160pp. 5⅜ × 8½. (Available in U.S. only) 25253-1 Pa. $4.95

HOW TO WRITE, Gertrude Stein. Gertrude Stein claimed anyone could understand her unconventional writing—here are clues to help. Fascinating improvisations, language experiments, explanations illuminate Stein's craft and the art of writing. Total of 414pp. 4⅜ × 6⅜. 23144-5 Pa. $6.95

ADVENTURES AT SEA IN THE GREAT AGE OF SAIL: Five Firsthand Narratives, edited by Elliot Snow. Rare true accounts of exploration, whaling, shipwreck, fierce natives, trade, shipboard life, more. 33 illustrations. Introduction. 353pp. 5⅜ × 8½. 25177-2 Pa. $8.95

THE HERBAL OR GENERAL HISTORY OF PLANTS, John Gerard. Classic descriptions of about 2,850 plants—with over 2,700 illustrations—includes Latin and English names, physical descriptions, varieties, time and place of growth, more. 2,706 illustrations. xlv + 1,678pp. 8½ × 12¼. 23147-X Cloth. $75.00

DOROTHY AND THE WIZARD IN OZ, L. Frank Baum. Dorothy and the Wizard visit the center of the Earth, where people are vegetables, glass houses grow and Oz characters reappear. Classic sequel to *Wizard of Oz*. 256pp. 5⅜ × 8. 24714-7 Pa. $5.95

SONGS OF EXPERIENCE: Facsimile Reproduction with 26 Plates in Full Color, William Blake. This facsimile of Blake's original "Illuminated Book" reproduces 26 full-color plates from a rare 1826 edition. Includes "The Tyger," "London," "Holy Thursday," and other immortal poems. 26 color plates. Printed text of poems. 48pp. 5¼ × 7. 24636-1 Pa. $3.95

SONGS OF INNOCENCE, William Blake. The first and most popular of Blake's famous "Illuminated Books," in a facsimile edition reproducing all 31 brightly colored plates. Additional printed text of each poem. 64pp. 5¼ × 7. 22764-2 Pa. $3.95

PRECIOUS STONES, Max Bauer. Classic, thorough study of diamonds, rubies, emeralds, garnets, etc.: physical character, occurrence, properties, use, similar topics. 20 plates, 8 in color. 94 figures. 659pp. 6⅛ × 9¼. 21910-0, 21911-9 Pa., Two-vol. set $15.90

ENCYCLOPEDIA OF VICTORIAN NEEDLEWORK, S. F. A. Caulfeild and Blanche Saward. Full, precise descriptions of stitches, techniques for dozens of needlecrafts—most exhaustive reference of its kind. Over 800 figures. Total of 679pp. 8⅛ × 11. Two volumes. Vol. 1 22800-2 Pa. $11.95
Vol. 2 22801-0 Pa. $11.95

THE MARVELOUS LAND OF OZ, L. Frank Baum. Second Oz book, the Scarecrow and Tin Woodman are back with hero named Tip, Oz magic. 136 illustrations. 287pp. 5⅜ × 8½. 20692-0 Pa. $5.95

WILD FOWL DECOYS, Joel Barber. Basic book on the subject, by foremost authority and collector. Reveals history of decoy making and rigging, place in American culture, different kinds of decoys, how to make them, and how to use them. 140 plates. 156pp. 7⅞ × 10¾. 20011-6 Pa. $8.95

HISTORY OF LACE, Mrs. Bury Palliser. Definitive, profusely illustrated chronicle of lace from earliest times to late 19th century. Laces of Italy, Greece, England, France, Belgium, etc. Landmark of needlework scholarship. 266 illustrations. 672pp. 6⅛ × 9¼. 24742-2 Pa. $14.95

ILLUSTRATED GUIDE TO SHAKER FURNITURE, Robert Meader. All furniture and appurtenances, with much on unknown local styles. 235 photos. 146pp. 9 × 12. 22819-3 Pa. $8.95

WHALE SHIPS AND WHALING: A Pictorial Survey, George Francis Dow. Over 200 vintage engravings, drawings, photographs of barks, brigs, cutters, other vessels. Also harpoons, lances, whaling guns, many other artifacts. Comprehensive text by foremost authority. 207 black-and-white illustrations. 288pp. 6 × 9. 24808-9 Pa. $9.95

THE BERTRAMS, Anthony Trollope. Powerful portrayal of blind self-will and thwarted ambition includes one of Trollope's most heartrending love stories. 497pp. 5⅜ × 8½. 25119-5 Pa. $9.95

ADVENTURES WITH A HAND LENS, Richard Headstrom. Clearly written guide to observing and studying flowers and grasses, fish scales, moth and insect wings, egg cases, buds, feathers, seeds, leaf scars, moss, molds, ferns, common crystals, etc.—all with an ordinary, inexpensive magnifying glass. 209 exact line drawings aid in your discoveries. 220pp. 5⅜ × 8½. 23330-8 Pa. $4.95

RODIN ON ART AND ARTISTS, Auguste Rodin. Great sculptor's candid, wide-ranging comments on meaning of art; great artists; relation of sculpture to poetry, painting, music; philosophy of life, more. 76 superb black-and-white illustrations of Rodin's sculpture, drawings and prints. 119pp. 8⅝ × 11¼. 24487-3 Pa. $7.95

FIFTY CLASSIC FRENCH FILMS, 1912–1982: A Pictorial Record, Anthony Slide. Memorable stills from Grand Illusion, Beauty and the Beast, Hiroshima, Mon Amour, many more. Credits, plot synopses, reviews, etc. 160pp. 8¼ × 11. 25256-6 Pa. $11.95

THE PRINCIPLES OF PSYCHOLOGY, William James. Famous long course complete, unabridged. Stream of thought, time perception, memory, experimental methods; great work decades ahead of its time. 94 figures. 1,391pp. 5⅜ × 8½. 20381-6, 20382-4 Pa., Two-vol. set $23.90

BODIES IN A BOOKSHOP, R. T. Campbell. Challenging mystery of blackmail and murder with ingenious plot and superbly drawn characters. In the best tradition of British suspense fiction. 192pp. 5⅜ × 8½. 24720-1 Pa. $4.95

CALLAS: PORTRAIT OF A PRIMA DONNA, George Jellinek. Renowned commentator on the musical scene chronicles incredible career and life of the most controversial, fascinating, influential operatic personality of our time. 64 black-and-white photographs. 416pp. 5⅜ × 8¼. 25047-4 Pa. $8.95

GEOMETRY, RELATIVITY AND THE FOURTH DIMENSION, Rudolph Rucker. Exposition of fourth dimension, concepts of relativity as Flatland characters continue adventures. Popular, easily followed yet accurate, profound. 141 illustrations. 133pp. 5⅜ × 8½. 23400-2 Pa. $4.95

HOUSEHOLD STORIES BY THE BROTHERS GRIMM, with pictures by Walter Crane. 53 classic stories—Rumpelstiltskin, Rapunzel, Hansel and Gretel, the Fisherman and his Wife, Snow White, Tom Thumb, Sleeping Beauty, Cinderella, and so much more—lavishly illustrated with original 19th century drawings. 114 illustrations. x + 269pp. 5⅜ × 8½. 21080-4 Pa. $4.95

SUNDIALS, Albert Waugh. Far and away the best, most thorough coverage of ideas, mathematics concerned, types, construction, adjusting anywhere. Over 100 illustrations. 230pp. 5⅜ × 8½. 22947-5 Pa. $5.95

PICTURE HISTORY OF THE NORMANDIE: With 190 Illustrations, Frank O. Braynard. Full story of legendary French ocean liner: Art Deco interiors, design innovations, furnishings, celebrities, maiden voyage, tragic fire, much more. Extensive text. 144pp. 8⅞ × 11¾. 25257-4 Pa. $10.95

THE FIRST AMERICAN COOKBOOK: A Facsimile of "American Cookery," 1796, Amelia Simmons. Facsimile of the first American-written cookbook published in the United States contains authentic recipes for colonial favorites—pumpkin pudding, winter squash pudding, spruce beer, Indian slapjacks, and more. Introductory Essay and Glossary of colonial cooking terms. 80pp. 5⅜ × 8½. 24710-4 Pa. $3.50

101 PUZZLES IN THOUGHT AND LOGIC, C. R. Wylie, Jr. Solve murders and robberies, find out which fishermen are liars, how a blind man could possibly identify a color—purely by your own reasoning! 107pp. 5⅜ × 8½. 20367-0 Pa. $2.50

ANCIENT EGYPTIAN MYTHS AND LEGENDS, Lewis Spence. Examines animism, totemism, fetishism, creation myths, deities, alchemy, art and magic, other topics. Over 50 illustrations. 432pp. 5⅜ × 8½. 26525-0 Pa. $8.95

ANTHROPOLOGY AND MODERN LIFE, Franz Boas. Great anthropologist's classic treatise on race and culture. Introduction by Ruth Bunzel. Only inexpensive paperback edition. 255pp. 5⅜ × 8½. 25245-0 Pa. $6.95

THE TALE OF PETER RABBIT, Beatrix Potter. The inimitable Peter's terrifying adventure in Mr. McGregor's garden, with all 27 wonderful, full-color Potter illustrations. 55pp. 4¼ × 5½. (Available in U.S. only) 22827-4 Pa. $1.75

THREE PROPHETIC SCIENCE FICTION NOVELS, H. G. Wells. *When the Sleeper Wakes, A Story of the Days to Come* and *The Time Machine* (full version). 335pp. 5⅜ × 8½. (Available in U.S. only) 20605-X Pa. $6.95

APICIUS COOKERY AND DINING IN IMPERIAL ROME, edited and translated by Joseph Dommers Vehling. Oldest known cookbook in existence offers readers a clear picture of what foods Romans ate, how they prepared them, etc. 49 illustrations. 301pp. 6⅛ × 9¼. 23563-7 Pa. $7.95

SHAKESPEARE LEXICON AND QUOTATION DICTIONARY, Alexander Schmidt. Full definitions, locations, shades of meaning of every word in plays and poems. More than 50,000 exact quotations. 1,485pp. 6½ × 9¼. 22726-X, 22727-8 Pa., Two-vol. set $31.90

THE WORLD'S GREAT SPEECHES, edited by Lewis Copeland and Lawrence W. Lamm. Vast collection of 278 speeches from Greeks to 1970. Powerful and effective models; unique look at history. 842pp. 5⅜ × 8½. 20468-5 Pa. $12.95

THE BLUE FAIRY BOOK, Andrew Lang. The first, most famous collection, with many familiar tales: Little Red Riding Hood, Aladdin and the Wonderful Lamp, Puss in Boots, Sleeping Beauty, Hansel and Gretel, Rumpelstiltskin; 37 in all. 138 illustrations. 390pp. 5⅜ × 8½. 21437-0 Pa. $6.95

THE STORY OF THE CHAMPIONS OF THE ROUND TABLE, Howard Pyle. Sir Launcelot, Sir Tristram and Sir Percival in spirited adventures of love and triumph retold in Pyle's inimitable style. 50 drawings, 31 full-page. xviii + 329pp. 6½ × 9¼. 21883-X Pa. $7.95

THE MYTHS OF THE NORTH AMERICAN INDIANS, Lewis Spence. Myths and legends of the Algonquins, Iroquois, Pawnees and Sioux with comprehensive historical and ethnological commentary. 36 illustrations. 5⅜ × 8½.
25967-6 Pa. $8.95

GREAT DINOSAUR HUNTERS AND THEIR DISCOVERIES, Edwin H. Colbert. Fascinating, lavishly illustrated chronicle of dinosaur research, 1820's to 1960. Achievements of Cope, Marsh, Brown, Buckland, Mantell, Huxley, many others. 384pp. 5¼ × 8¼. 24701-5 Pa. $7.95

THE TASTEMAKERS, Russell Lynes. Informal, illustrated social history of American taste 1850's–1950's. First popularized categories Highbrow, Lowbrow, Middlebrow. 129 illustrations. New (1979) afterword. 384pp. 6 × 9.
23993-4 Pa. $8.95

DOUBLE CROSS PURPOSES, Ronald A. Knox. A treasure hunt in the Scottish Highlands, an old map, unidentified corpse, surprise discoveries keep reader guessing in this cleverly intricate tale of financial skullduggery. 2 black-and-white maps. 320pp. 5⅜ × 8½. (Available in U.S. only) 25032-6 Pa. $6.95

AUTHENTIC VICTORIAN DECORATION AND ORNAMENTATION IN FULL COLOR: 46 Plates from "Studies in Design," Christopher Dresser. Superb full-color lithographs reproduced from rare original portfolio of a major Victorian designer. 48pp. 9¼ × 12¼. 25083-0 Pa. $7.95

PRIMITIVE ART, Franz Boas. Remains the best text ever prepared on subject, thoroughly discussing Indian, African, Asian, Australian, and, especially, Northern American primitive art. Over 950 illustrations show ceramics, masks, totem poles, weapons, textiles, paintings, much more. 376pp. 5⅜ × 8. 20025-6 Pa. $7.95

SIDELIGHTS ON RELATIVITY, Albert Einstein. Unabridged republication of two lectures delivered by the great physicist in 1920–21. *Ether and Relativity* and *Geometry and Experience*. Elegant ideas in non-mathematical form, accessible to intelligent layman. vi + 56pp. 5⅜ × 8½. 24511-X Pa. $2.95

THE WIT AND HUMOR OF OSCAR WILDE, edited by Alvin Redman. More than 1,000 ripostes, paradoxes, wisecracks: Work is the curse of the drinking classes, I can resist everything except temptation, etc. 258pp. 5⅜ × 8½. 20602-5 Pa. $4.95

ADVENTURES WITH A MICROSCOPE, Richard Headstrom. 59 adventures with clothing fibers, protozoa, ferns and lichens, roots and leaves, much more. 142 illustrations. 232pp. 5⅜ × 8½. 23471-1 Pa. $3.95

PLANTS OF THE BIBLE, Harold N. Moldenke and Alma L. Moldenke. Standard reference to all 230 plants mentioned in Scriptures. Latin name, biblical reference, uses, modern identity, much more. Unsurpassed encyclopedic resource for scholars, botanists, nature lovers, students of Bible. Bibliography. Indexes. 123 black-and-white illustrations. 384pp. 6 × 9. 25069-5 Pa. $8.95

FAMOUS AMERICAN WOMEN: A Biographical Dictionary from Colonial Times to the Present, Robert McHenry, ed. From Pocahontas to Rosa Parks, 1,035 distinguished American women documented in separate biographical entries. Accurate, up-to-date data, numerous categories, spans 400 years. Indices. 493pp. 6½ × 9¼. 24523-3 Pa. $10.95

THE FABULOUS INTERIORS OF THE GREAT OCEAN LINERS IN HISTORIC PHOTOGRAPHS, William H. Miller, Jr. Some 200 superb photographs capture exquisite interiors of world's great "floating palaces"—1890's to 1980's: Titanic, Ile de France, Queen Elizabeth, United States, Europa, more. Approx. 200 black-and-white photographs. Captions. Text. Introduction. 160pp. 8⅜ × 11¼. 24756-2 Pa. $9.95

THE GREAT LUXURY LINERS, 1927–1954: A Photographic Record, William H. Miller, Jr. Nostalgic tribute to heyday of ocean liners. 186 photos of Ile de France, Normandie, Leviathan, Queen Elizabeth, United States, many others. Interior and exterior views. Introduction. Captions. 160pp. 9 × 12. 24056-8 Pa. $10.95

A NATURAL HISTORY OF THE DUCKS, John Charles Phillips. Great landmark of ornithology offers complete detailed coverage of nearly 200 species and subspecies of ducks: gadwall, sheldrake, merganser, pintail, many more. 74 full-color plates, 102 black-and-white. Bibliography. Total of 1,920pp. 8⅜ × 11¼. 25141-1, 25142-X Cloth. Two-vol. set $100.00

THE SEAWEED HANDBOOK: An Illustrated Guide to Seaweeds from North Carolina to Canada, Thomas F. Lee. Concise reference covers 78 species. Scientific and common names, habitat, distribution, more. Finding keys for easy identification. 224pp. 5⅜ × 8½. 25215-9 Pa. $6.95

THE TEN BOOKS OF ARCHITECTURE: The 1755 Leoni Edition, Leon Battista Alberti. Rare classic helped introduce the glories of ancient architecture to the Renaissance. 68 black-and-white plates. 336pp. 8⅜ × 11¼. 25239-6 Pa. $14.95

MISS MACKENZIE, Anthony Trollope. Minor masterpieces by Victorian master unmasks many truths about life in 19th-century England. First inexpensive edition in years. 392pp. 5⅜ × 8½. 25201-9 Pa. $8.95

THE RIME OF THE ANCIENT MARINER, Gustave Doré, Samuel Taylor Coleridge. Dramatic engravings considered by many to be his greatest work. The terrifying space of the open sea, the storms and whirlpools of an unknown ocean, the ice of Antarctica, more—all rendered in a powerful, chilling manner. Full text. 38 plates. 77pp. 9¼ × 12. 22305-1 Pa. $4.95

THE EXPEDITIONS OF ZEBULON MONTGOMERY PIKE, Zebulon Montgomery Pike. Fascinating first-hand accounts (1805–6) of exploration of Mississippi River, Indian wars, capture by Spanish dragoons, much more. 1,088pp. 5⅜ × 8½. 25254-X, 25255-8 Pa. Two-vol. set $25.90

A CONCISE HISTORY OF PHOTOGRAPHY: Third Revised Edition, Helmut Gernsheim. Best one-volume history—camera obscura, photochemistry, daguerreotypes, evolution of cameras, film, more. Also artistic aspects—landscape, portraits, fine art, etc. 281 black-and-white photographs. 26 in color. 176pp. 8⅜ × 11¼. 25128-4 Pa. $13.95

THE DORÉ BIBLE ILLUSTRATIONS, Gustave Doré. 241 detailed plates from the Bible: the Creation scenes, Adam and Eve, Flood, Babylon, battle sequences, life of Jesus, etc. Each plate is accompanied by the verses from the King James version of the Bible. 241pp. 9 × 12. 23004-X Pa. $9.95

WANDERINGS IN WEST AFRICA, Richard F. Burton. Great Victorian scholar/adventurer's invaluable descriptions of African tribal rituals, fetishism, culture, art, much more. Fascinating 19th-century account. 624pp. 5⅜ × 8½. 26890-X Pa. $12.95

FLATLAND, E. A. Abbott. Intriguing and enormously popular science-fiction classic explores the complexities of trying to survive as a two-dimensional being in a three-dimensional world. Amusingly illustrated by the author. 16 illustrations. 103pp. 5⅜ × 8½. 20001-9 Pa. $2.50

THE HISTORY OF THE LEWIS AND CLARK EXPEDITION, Meriwether Lewis and William Clark, edited by Elliott Coues. Classic edition of Lewis and Clark's day-by-day journals that later became the basis for U.S. claims to Oregon and the West. Accurate and invaluable geographical, botanical, biological, meteorological and anthropological material. Total of 1,508pp. 5⅜ × 8½.
21268-8, 21269-6, 21270-X Pa. Three-vol. set $26.85

LANGUAGE, TRUTH AND LOGIC, Alfred J. Ayer. Famous, clear introduction to Vienna, Cambridge schools of Logical Positivism. Role of philosophy, elimination of metaphysics, nature of analysis, etc. 160pp. 5⅜ × 8½. (Available in U.S. and Canada only) 20010-8 Pa. $3.95

MATHEMATICS FOR THE NONMATHEMATICIAN, Morris Kline. Detailed, college-level treatment of mathematics in cultural and historical context, with numerous exercises. For liberal arts students. Preface. Recommended Reading Lists. Tables. Index. Numerous black-and-white figures. xvi + 641pp. 5⅜ × 8½.
24823-2 Pa. $11.95

HANDBOOK OF PICTORIAL SYMBOLS, Rudolph Modley. 3,250 signs and symbols, many systems in full; official or heavy commercial use. Arranged by subject. Most in Pictorial Archive series. 143pp. 8⅛ × 11. 23357-X Pa. $6.95

INCIDENTS OF TRAVEL IN YUCATAN, John L. Stephens. Classic (1843) exploration of jungles of Yucatan, looking for evidences of Maya civilization. Travel adventures, Mexican and Indian culture, etc. Total of 669pp. 5⅜ × 8½.
20926-1, 20927-X Pa., Two-vol. set $11.90

DEGAS: An Intimate Portrait, Ambroise Vollard. Charming, anecdotal memoir by famous art dealer of one of the greatest 19th-century French painters. 14 black-and-white illustrations. Introduction by Harold L. Van Doren. 96pp. 5⅜ × 8½.

25131-4 Pa. $4.95

PERSONAL NARRATIVE OF A PILGRIMAGE TO ALMANDINAH AND MECCAH, Richard Burton. Great travel classic by remarkably colorful personality. Burton, disguised as a Moroccan, visited sacred shrines of Islam, narrowly escaping death. 47 illustrations. 959pp. 5⅜ × 8½.   21217-3, 21218-1 Pa., Two-vol. set $19.90

PHRASE AND WORD ORIGINS, A. H. Holt. Entertaining, reliable, modern study of more than 1,200 colorful words, phrases, origins and histories. Much unexpected information. 254pp. 5⅜ × 8½.   20758-7 Pa. $5.95

THE RED THUMB MARK, R. Austin Freeman. In this first Dr. Thorndyke case, the great scientific detective draws fascinating conclusions from the nature of a single fingerprint. Exciting story, authentic science. 320pp. 5⅜ × 8½. (Available in U.S. only)   25210-8 Pa. $6.95

AN EGYPTIAN HIEROGLYPHIC DICTIONARY, E. A. Wallis Budge. Monumental work containing about 25,000 words or terms that occur in texts ranging from 3000 B.C. to 600 A.D. Each entry consists of a transliteration of the word, the word in hieroglyphs, and the meaning in English. 1,314pp. 6⅜ × 10.

23615-3, 23616-1 Pa., Two-vol. set $35.90

THE COMPLEAT STRATEGYST: Being a Primer on the Theory of Games of Strategy, J. D. Williams. Highly entertaining classic describes, with many illustrated examples, how to select best strategies in conflict situations. Prefaces. Appendices. xvi + 268pp. 5⅜ × 8½.   25101-2 Pa. $6.95

THE ROAD TO OZ, L. Frank Baum. Dorothy meets the Shaggy Man, little Button-Bright and the Rainbow's beautiful daughter in this delightful trip to the magical Land of Oz. 272pp. 5⅜ × 8.   25208-6 Pa. $5.95

POINT AND LINE TO PLANE, Wassily Kandinsky. Seminal exposition of role of point, line, other elements in non-objective painting. Essential to understanding 20th-century art. 127 illustrations. 192pp. 6½ × 9¼.   23808-3 Pa. $5.95

LADY ANNA, Anthony Trollope. Moving chronicle of Countess Lovel's bitter struggle to win for herself and daughter Anna their rightful rank and fortune— perhaps at cost of sanity itself. 384pp. 5⅜ × 8½.   24669-8 Pa. $8.95

EGYPTIAN MAGIC, E. A. Wallis Budge. Sums up all that is known about magic in Ancient Egypt: the role of magic in controlling the gods, powerful amulets that warded off evil spirits, scarabs of immortality, use of wax images, formulas and spells, the secret name, much more. 253pp. 5⅜ × 8½.   22681-6 Pa. $4.50

THE DANCE OF SIVA, Ananda Coomaraswamy. Preeminent authority unfolds the vast metaphysic of India: the revelation of her art, conception of the universe, social organization, etc. 27 reproductions of art masterpieces. 192pp. 5⅜ × 8½.

24817-8 Pa. $5.95

CHRISTMAS CUSTOMS AND TRADITIONS, Clement A. Miles. Origin, evolution, significance of religious, secular practices. Caroling, gifts, yule logs, much more. Full, scholarly yet fascinating; non-sectarian. 400pp. 5⅜ × 8½.
23354-5 Pa. $6.95

THE HUMAN FIGURE IN MOTION, Eadweard Muybridge. More than 4,500 stopped-action photos, in action series, showing undraped men, women, children jumping, lying down, throwing, sitting, wrestling, carrying, etc. 390pp. 7⅞ × 10⅝.
20204-6 Cloth. $24.95

THE MAN WHO WAS THURSDAY, Gilbert Keith Chesterton. Witty, fast-paced novel about a club of anarchists in turn-of-the-century London. Brilliant social, religious, philosophical speculations. 128pp. 5⅜ × 8½.
25121-7 Pa. $3.95

A CEZANNE SKETCHBOOK: Figures, Portraits, Landscapes and Still Lifes, Paul Cezanne. Great artist experiments with tonal effects, light, mass, other qualities in over 100 drawings. A revealing view of developing master painter, precursor of Cubism. 102 black-and-white illustrations. 144pp. 8¾ × 6⅝.
24790-2 Pa. $6.95

AN ENCYCLOPEDIA OF BATTLES: Accounts of Over 1,560 Battles from 1479 B.C. to the Present, David Eggenberger. Presents essential details of every major battle in recorded history, from the first battle of Megiddo in 1479 B.C. to Grenada in 1984. List of Battle Maps. New Appendix covering the years 1967–1984. Index. 99 illustrations. 544pp. 6½ × 9¼.
24913-1 Pa. $14.95

AN ETYMOLOGICAL DICTIONARY OF MODERN ENGLISH, Ernest Weekley. Richest, fullest work, by foremost British lexicographer. Detailed word histories. Inexhaustible. Total of 856pp. 6½ × 9¼.
21873-2, 21874-0 Pa., Two-vol. set $19.90

WEBSTER'S AMERICAN MILITARY BIOGRAPHIES, edited by Robert McHenry. Over 1,000 figures who shaped 3 centuries of American military history. Detailed biographies of Nathan Hale, Douglas MacArthur, Mary Hallaren, others. Chronologies of engagements, more. Introduction. Addenda. 1,033 entries in alphabetical order. xi + 548pp. 6½ × 9¼. (Available in U.S. only)
24758-9 Pa. $13.95

LIFE IN ANCIENT EGYPT, Adolf Erman. Detailed older account, with much not in more recent books: domestic life, religion, magic, medicine, commerce, and whatever else needed for complete picture. Many illustrations. 597pp. 5⅜ × 8½.
22632-8 Pa. $8.95

HISTORIC COSTUME IN PICTURES, Braun & Schneider. Over 1,450 costumed figures shown, covering a wide variety of peoples: kings, emperors, nobles, priests, servants, soldiers, scholars, townsfolk, peasants, merchants, courtiers, cavaliers, and more. 256pp. 8⅜ × 11¼.
23150-X Pa. $9.95

THE NOTEBOOKS OF LEONARDO DA VINCI, edited by J. P. Richter. Extracts from manuscripts reveal great genius; on painting, sculpture, anatomy, sciences, geography, etc. Both Italian and English. 186 ms. pages reproduced, plus 500 additional drawings, including studies for *Last Supper, Sforza* monument, etc. 860pp. 7⅞ × 10¾. (Available in U.S. only) 22572-0, 22573-9 Pa., Two-vol. set $31.90

THE ART NOUVEAU STYLE BOOK OF ALPHONSE MUCHA: All 72 Plates from "Documents Decoratifs" in Original Color, Alphonse Mucha. Rare copyright-free design portfolio by high priest of Art Nouveau. Jewelry, wallpaper, stained glass, furniture, figure studies, plant and animal motifs, etc. Only complete one-volume edition. 80pp. 9⅜ × 12¼. 24044-4 Pa. $9.95

ANIMALS: 1,419 COPYRIGHT-FREE ILLUSTRATIONS OF MAMMALS, BIRDS, FISH, INSECTS, ETC., edited by Jim Harter. Clear wood engravings present, in extremely lifelike poses, over 1,000 species of animals. One of the most extensive pictorial sourcebooks of its kind. Captions. Index. 284pp. 9 × 12. 23766-4 Pa. $9.95

OBELISTS FLY HIGH, C. Daly King. Masterpiece of American detective fiction, long out of print, involves murder on a 1935 transcontinental flight—"a very thrilling story"—NY Times. Unabridged and unaltered republication of the edition published by William Collins Sons & Co. Ltd., London, 1935. 288pp. 5⅜ × 8½. (Available in U.S. only) 25036-9 Pa. $5.95

VICTORIAN AND EDWARDIAN FASHION: A Photographic Survey, Alison Gernsheim. First fashion history completely illustrated by contemporary photographs. Full text plus 235 photos, 1840–1914, in which many celebrities appear. 240pp. 6½ × 9¼. 24205-6 Pa. $8.95

THE ART OF THE FRENCH ILLUSTRATED BOOK, 1700–1914, Gordon N. Ray. Over 630 superb book illustrations by Fragonard, Delacroix, Daumier, Doré, Grandville, Manet, Mucha, Steinlen, Toulouse-Lautrec and many others. Preface. Introduction. 633 halftones. Indices of artists, authors & titles, binders and provenances. Appendices. Bibliography. 608pp. 8⅜ × 11¼. 25086-5 Pa. $24.95

THE WONDERFUL WIZARD OF OZ, L. Frank Baum. Facsimile in full color of America's finest children's classic. 143 illustrations by W. W. Denslow. 267pp. 5⅜ × 8½. 20691-2 Pa. $7.95

FOLLOWING THE EQUATOR: A Journey Around the World, Mark Twain. Great writer's 1897 account of circumnavigating the globe by steamship. Ironic humor, keen observations, vivid and fascinating descriptions of exotic places. 197 illustrations. 720pp. 5⅜ × 8½. 26113-1 Pa. $15.95

THE FRIENDLY STARS, Martha Evans Martin & Donald Howard Menzel. Classic text marshalls the stars together in an engaging, non-technical survey, presenting them as sources of beauty in night sky. 23 illustrations. Foreword. 2 star charts. Index. 147pp. 5⅜ × 8½. 21099-5 Pa. $3.95

FADS AND FALLACIES IN THE NAME OF SCIENCE, Martin Gardner. Fair, witty appraisal of cranks, quacks, and quackeries of science and pseudoscience: hollow earth, Velikovsky, orgone energy, Dianetics, flying saucers, Bridey Murphy, food and medical fads, etc. Revised, expanded In the Name of Science. "A very able and even-tempered presentation."—The New Yorker. 363pp. 5⅜ × 8. 20394-8 Pa. $6.95

ANCIENT EGYPT: ITS CULTURE AND HISTORY, J. E Manchip White. From pre-dynastics through Ptolemies: society, history, political structure, religion, daily life, literature, cultural heritage. 48 plates. 217pp. 5⅜ × 8½. 22548-8 Pa. $5.95

SIR HARRY HOTSPUR OF HUMBLETHWAITE, Anthony Trollope. Incisive, unconventional psychological study of a conflict between a wealthy baronet, his idealistic daughter, and their scapegrace cousin. The 1870 novel in its first inexpensive edition in years. 250pp. 5⅜ × 8½. 24953-0 Pa. $6.95

LASERS AND HOLOGRAPHY, Winston E. Kock. Sound introduction to burgeoning field, expanded (1981) for second edition. Wave patterns, coherence, lasers, diffraction, zone plates, properties of holograms, recent advances. 84 illustrations. 160pp. 5⅜ × 8¼. (Except in United Kingdom) 24041-X Pa. $3.95

INTRODUCTION TO ARTIFICIAL INTELLIGENCE: SECOND, EN-LARGED EDITION, Philip C. Jackson, Jr. Comprehensive survey of artificial intelligence—the study of how machines (computers) can be made to act intelligently. Includes introductory and advanced material. Extensive notes updating the main text. 132 black-and-white illustrations. 512pp. 5⅜ × 8½. 24864-X Pa. $8.95

HISTORY OF INDIAN AND INDONESIAN ART, Ananda K. Coomaraswamy. Over 400 illustrations illuminate classic study of Indian art from earliest Harappa finds to early 20th century. Provides philosophical, religious and social insights. 304pp. 6⅜ × 9⅜. 25005-9 Pa. $11.95

THE GOLEM, Gustav Meyrink. Most famous supernatural novel in modern European literature, set in Ghetto of Old Prague around 1890. Compelling story of mystical experiences, strange transformations, profound terror. 13 black-and-white illustrations. 224pp. 5⅜ × 8½. (Available in U.S. only) 25025-3 Pa. $6.95

PICTORIAL ENCYCLOPEDIA OF HISTORIC ARCHITECTURAL PLANS, DETAILS AND ELEMENTS: With 1,880 Line Drawings of Arches, Domes, Doorways, Facades, Gables, Windows, etc., John Theodore Haneman. Sourcebook of inspiration for architects, designers, others. Bibliography. Captions. 141pp. 9 × 12. 24605-1 Pa. $7.95

BENCHLEY LOST AND FOUND, Robert Benchley. Finest humor from early 30's, about pet peeves, child psychologists, post office and others. Mostly unavailable elsewhere. 73 illustrations by Peter Arno and others. 183pp. 5⅜ × 8½. 22410-4 Pa. $4.95

ERTÉ GRAPHICS, Erté. Collection of striking color graphics: *Seasons, Alphabet, Numerals, Aces* and *Precious Stones*. 50 plates, including 4 on covers. 48pp. 9⅜ × 12¼. 23580-7 Pa. $7.95

THE JOURNAL OF HENRY D. THOREAU, edited by Bradford Torrey, F. H. Allen. Complete reprinting of 14 volumes, 1837–61, over two million words; the sourcebooks for *Walden*, etc. Definitive. All original sketches, plus 75 photographs. 1,804pp. 8½ × 12¼. 20312-3, 20313-1 Cloth., Two-vol. set $125.00

CASTLES: THEIR CONSTRUCTION AND HISTORY, Sidney Toy. Traces castle development from ancient roots. Nearly 200 photographs and drawings illustrate moats, keeps, baileys, many other features. Caernarvon, Dover Castles, Hadrian's Wall, Tower of London, dozens more. 256pp. 5⅜ × 8¼. 24898-4 Pa. $6.95

AMERICAN CLIPPER SHIPS: 1833–1858, Octavius T. Howe & Frederick C. Matthews. Fully-illustrated, encyclopedic review of 352 clipper ships from the period of America's greatest maritime supremacy. Introduction. 109 halftones. 5 black-and-white line illustrations. Index. Total of 928pp. 5⅜ × 8½.
25115-2, 25116-0 Pa., Two-vol. set $17.90

TOWARDS A NEW ARCHITECTURE, Le Corbusier. Pioneering manifesto by great architect, near legendary founder of "International School." Technical and aesthetic theories, views on industry, economics, relation of form to function, "mass-production spirit," much more. Profusely illustrated. Unabridged translation of 13th French edition. Introduction by Frederick Etchells. 320pp. 6⅛ × 9¼. (Available in U.S. only)
25023-7 Pa. $8.95

THE BOOK OF KELLS, edited by Blanche Cirker. Inexpensive collection of 32 full-color, full-page plates from the greatest illuminated manuscript of the Middle Ages, painstakingly reproduced from rare facsimile edition. Publisher's Note. Captions. 32pp. 9⅜ × 12¼.
24345-1 Pa. $4.95

BEST SCIENCE FICTION STORIES OF H. G. WELLS, H. G. Wells. Full novel *The Invisible Man*, plus 17 short stories: "The Crystal Egg," "Aepyornis Island," "The Strange Orchid," etc. 303pp. 5⅜ × 8½. (Available in U.S. only)
21531-8 Pa. $6.95

AMERICAN SAILING SHIPS: Their Plans and History, Charles G. Davis. Photos, construction details of schooners, frigates, clippers, other sailcraft of 18th to early 20th centuries—plus entertaining discourse on design, rigging, nautical lore, much more. 137 black-and-white illustrations. 240pp. 6⅛ × 9¼.
24658-2 Pa. $6.95

ENTERTAINING MATHEMATICAL PUZZLES, Martin Gardner. Selection of author's favorite conundrums involving arithmetic, money, speed, etc., with lively commentary. Complete solutions. 112pp. 5⅜ × 8½.
25211-6 Pa. $2.95

THE WILL TO BELIEVE, HUMAN IMMORTALITY, William James. Two books bound together. Effect of irrational on logical, and arguments for human immortality. 402pp. 5⅜ × 8½.
20291-7 Pa. $7.95

THE HAUNTED MONASTERY and THE CHINESE MAZE MURDERS, Robert Van Gulik. 2 full novels by Van Gulik continue adventures of Judge Dee and his companions. An evil Taoist monastery, seemingly supernatural events; overgrown topiary maze that hides strange crimes. Set in 7th-century China. 27 illustrations. 328pp. 5⅜ × 8½.
23502-5 Pa. $6.95

CELEBRATED CASES OF JUDGE DEE (DEE GOONG AN), translated by Robert Van Gulik. Authentic 18th-century Chinese detective novel; Dee and associates solve three interlocked cases. Led to Van Gulik's own stories with same characters. Extensive introduction. 9 illustrations. 237pp. 5⅜ × 8½.
23337-5 Pa. $5.95

Prices subject to change without notice.

Available at your book dealer or write for free catalog to Dept. GI, Dover Publications, Inc., 31 East 2nd St., Mineola, N.Y. 11501. Dover publishes more than 175 books each year on science, elementary and advanced mathematics, biology, music, art, literary history, social sciences and other areas.